Finding Fertile Ground

Identifying Extraordinary Opportunities for New Ventures

Finding Fertile Ground

Identifying Extraordinary Opportunities for New Ventures

Scott A. Shane
Department of Economics
Weatherhead School of Management
Case Western Reserve University

Ideas. Action. Impact.
Wharton School Publishing

A CIP record of this book can be obtained from the Library of Congress

Publisher: Tim Moore
Executive editor: Jim Boyd
Editorial/production supervision: Patty Donovan (Pine Tree Composition, Inc.)
Cover designer: Chuti Prosertsith
Art director: Gail Cocker-Bogusz
Marketing manager: Martin Litkowski
International marketing manager: Tim Galligan
Manufacturing coordinator: Dan Uhrig
Editoral assistant: Michelle Vincenti
Full-service production manager: Kristy Hart

Ideas. Action. Impact.
Wharton School
Publishing

© 2005 by Pearson Education, Inc.
Publishing as Wharton School Publishing
Upper Saddle River, New Jersey 07458

**Wharton School Publishing offers excellent discounts on this book
when ordered in quantity for bulk purchases or special sales.
For more information, please contact: U.S. Corporate and
Government Sales, 1-800-382-3419,
corpsales@pearsontechgroup.com. For sales outside of the U.S.,
please contact: International Sales, 1-317-581-3793,
international@pearsontechgroup.com.**

Printed in the United States of America

First Printing

ISBN 0-13-142398-3

Pearson Education LTD.
Pearson Education Australia PTY, Limited
Pearson Education Singapore, Pte. Ltd.
Pearson Education North Asia Ltd.
Pearson Education Canada, Ltd.
Pearson Educación de Mexico, S.A. de C.V.
Pearson Education—Japan
Pearson Education Malaysia, Pte. Ltd.

Ideas. Action. Impact.
**Wharton School
Publishing**

C. K. Prahalad
THE FORTUNE AT THE BOTTOM OF THE PYRAMID
Eradicating Poverty Through Profits

Yoram (Jerry)Wind, Colin Crook, with Robert Gunther
THE POWER OF IMPOSSIBLE THINKING
Transform the Business of Your Life and the Life of Your Business

Scott A. Shane
FINDING FERTILE GROUND
Identifying Extraordinary Opportunities for New Ventures

**To Lynne, for supporting my writing
and everything else that I do**

CONTENTS

Acknowledgments   xi

Introduction   xv

Chapter 1:   Selecting the Right Industry   1

Chapter 2:   Identifying Valuable Opportunities   19

Chapter 3:   Managing Technological Evolution   39

Chapter 4:   Identifying and Satisfying Real Market Needs   63

Chapter 5:   Understanding Customer Adoption   81

Chapter 6:   Exploiting Established Company Weaknesses   101

Chapter 7:   Managing Intellectual Property   125

Chapter 8:   Appropriating the Returns to Innovation   147

Chapter 9:   Choosing the Right
                 Organizational Form   163

Chapter 10:   Managing Risk
                 and Uncertainty   177

                 Conclusions   199

                 Index   215

ACKNOWLEDGMENTS

I decided to write this book after teaching a course in technology entrepreneurship to MBA students at Massachusetts Institute of Technology and at the University of Maryland. The class was very popular because it demonstrated how to start a new business that had a high probability of going public or becoming a high growth private enterprise. However, finding something for the classes to read on the topic was a challenge. There was no book that discussed high-technology entrepreneurship in a way that showed people how to identify a business opportunity to exploit a new technology success-fully. As a result, I had to search a wide range of academic articles to find the materials that I needed to explain the key issues identifying an opportunity to start a successful technology company. My interac-tions with the students, and, in particular, the questions that they asked me about the articles that they read and the lectures that they heard provided the basis for the material in this book. Therefore, I would like to thank all of those students for their intellectual

curiosity, which helped me figure out what aspiring technology entrepreneurs really need to know about how to develop an effective business concept for a new technology business.

I would also like to thank all of the scholars and practitioners on
whose work I have drawn to provide the framework for this book.
While the ideas presented in this book were influenced by many people, several are particularly important: David Audretsch, Amar
Bhide, Clay Christiansen, Richard Foster, Alvin Klevorick, Richard
Levin, Geoffrey Moore, Richard Nelson, Everett Rogers, David
Teece, and Jim Utterback. The books and articles that these people
wrote were extremely valuable in helping me to develop the ideas
presented in this book.

Over the years, I have had a variety of collaborators who have
taught me a great deal about technology entrepreneurship. In particular, Robert Baron, Dan Cable, Frederic Delmar, Jon Eckhardt, Bill
Gartner, Ian MacMillan, and S. Venkataraman stand out. Other colleagues have generously given their time to discuss entrepreneurship
with me, thereby shaping many of the ideas in this book, including
Bob Baum, Terry Blum, Per Davidsson, Brent Goldfarb, David
Kirsch, Rudy Lamone, Ed Roberts, Saras Sarasvathy, Scott Stern,
Rama Velamuri, and Eric Von Hippel. I would like to thank all of
them. This book would not have been possible without the help of
these people.

I would also like to thank my editor, Jim Boyd. Not only did Jim
believe in the vision that I had of taking ideas developed by academics and thoughtful practitioners and turning them into a practical
book to help people become successful technology entrepreneurs,
but he was instrumental in shaping that vision. His efforts to help me
craft the right type of book, providing enough explanation and examples to educate readers without being too academic, were invaluable.

Last, I would like to thank my wife, Lynne, and daughter,
Hannah. Each of them helped me in their own ways. Hannah helped

me by being source of joy and inspiration (as well as an excellent play-mate when I needed breaks from writing). Lynne helped me by always being willing to discuss my work and give me feedback on it, as well as for encouraging me and supporting me in my efforts to create this book.

INTRODUCTION

We live in an entrepreneurial society in an entrepreneurial age. Surveys consistently rank the United States as one of the most entrepreneurial countries in the world. Moreover, the rate of new firm creation in the United States has grown dramatically since the mid-1970s. The number of organizations created each year has reached levels that have not been seen since records have been kept (the past 150 years). As a result of this entrepreneurial orientation, approximately 4 percent of the U.S. labor force is involved in starting a new company every year—more than the number of people getting married or having children each year![1]—bringing the total of business owners to about 13 percent of the nonagricultural labor force.[2]

In addition, our economy operates through a process of creative destruction. Every year large, established corporations are toppled from their positions of dominance by start-up companies whose new ways of doing business render the competitive advantages of established firms obsolete. A glance at the pages of the Fortune 500 over the past several decades indicates incredible fluidity among the listed companies. Very few Fortune 500 companies remain Fortune 500 companies for more than a decade or two. Every year new companies go public and use the capital that they raise to challenge established industry leaders. The tendency for our economy to create new firms that topple giants in their industries has made successful entrepreneurs such as Jeff Bezos, Bill Gates, Michael Dell, Steve Jobs, Sam Walton, and Meg Whitman, who have founded these giant-killers, heroes and household names.

Despite the entrepreneurial orientation of our economy, and the iconlike status of successful entrepreneurs, most of the entrepreneurial activity that takes place in our economy is actually a dismal failure. Much like the typical lottery ticket buyer who dreams of being the jackpot winner, but ends up holding a handful of losing tickets, the typical entrepreneurial effort ends in a business closure that was not financially beneficial to its founder. Forty percent of all new businesses started in the United States do not live one year, more than two-thirds of new business created in this country die before their fifth birthday, and only 25 percent of new businesses survive eight years. Moreover, most entrepreneurs make very little money. On average, an entrepreneur who continues a business for 10 years—the elite few who manage to survive that long—make only 65 percent of the value of the real earnings that they made in their previous employment, including their return on stock ownership in their new company.[3]

The Purpose of This Book

Obviously, something separates successful entrepreneurs from the masses who try their hand at this activity every year. This book identifies the key difference between the successes and the masses—the selection of the right business concept to exploit a valuable opportunity. The central goal of this book is to provide you, as a potential or actual technology entrepreneur, with the tools necessary to identify the right business concept to exploit a valuable opportunity when you establish your business.

Of course, the information provided in this book will not guarantee you success in a high-technology entrepreneurship. Much in the same way as having the right form for a jump shot will not guarantee that a basketball player will earn $20 million per year in the NBA, understanding what makes a business a good one for an entrepreneur to start will not guarantee that you, as an entrepreneur, will take a start-up public, replace the leading companies in an industry, or even be profitable. However, understanding the information in this book, and following the rules that it outlines, will dramatically increase the probability of a successful outcome.

You probably noticed that the title of this book implies that it focuses on technology entrepreneurship, and I have not said anything about technology businesses yet. The title of the book is not wrong— the book is indeed about technology entrepreneurship—and this is the first lesson of being a successful entrepreneur. On average, entrepreneurs are more successful if they create high-technology start-ups than if they initiate low-technology start-ups. This is not to say that you cannot be successful if you start a low technology business. You only have to look to Sam Walton and Walmart to know that is not true.

However, being a successful entrepreneur involves playing the odds, not looking at extreme examples. Much like most professional gamblers know that they cannot guarantee they will win any given game they play at a casino in Las Vegas or Atlantic City, but play the games that have the best odds, most professional entrepreneurs play the opportunities that have the highest probability of generating profitable private companies or create new public companies. Professional entrepreneurs—serial entrepreneurs such as Jim Clark, who founded Netscape and Healtheon—and their professional investors, the venture capitalists who finance many of these firms, almost always focus on high technology businesses because they know that the odds of success are best with these kinds of companies. These professionals know, for example, that, over the past 25 years, the number one factor predicting the proportion of start-up firms in an industry that become one of the *Inc* 500 fastest growing companies or have gone public is the proportion of technical employees in the industry. They also know that the number one predictor of new business failure is the industry in which the firm is founded, with retail businesses and restaurants having extremely high failure rates.

Despite the clear effect of industry on the probability of new venture success, the typical entrepreneur starts a business in low-technology industry such as retail or restaurants, where the failure rate of new businesses is highest and the average profits are lowest. Unlike the successful entrepreneurs, typical entrepreneurs choose to start businesses in the wrong industries, making them very unlikely to be successful.

While this observation is disheartening because it illustrates how the majority of entrepreneurs set themselves up for failure, it is also instructive. It demonstrates that you can maximize your chances of success by following the example of professional entrepreneurs and their investors by choosing the right industries to enter, and ignoring the example of the mass of uninformed and unsuccessful entrepreneurs who select the wrong ones.

What I Mean by Technology

One thing that is important to clarify right at the outset of this book is what I mean by technology. In recent years, there has been a tendency for the media to use the word technology to mean information technology (IT). These days, when you turn on CNBC or read the *Wall Street Journal,* and you hear or see the word "technology" to describe something, it is usually in reference to IT companies. This book uses the word technology in a broader, more traditional sense.

Technology is the embodiment of knowledge in ways that make it possible to create new products, exploit new markets, use new ways of organizing, incorporate new raw materials, or use new processes to meet customer needs. Certainly, information technology—the use of zeros and ones in digital form on computers—is an important technology, but there are many other important technologies as well. Biologically based technologies, such as those used to create new drugs or to clean up pollution, are also important. Similarly, mechanically based technologies, such as those that make pumps or valves, matter. New materials, such as those in new ceramic composites, are valuable.

When I refer to technology in this book, I do not just mean simply information technology, though that is certainly one form of technology; I also mean new microorganisms, new mechanical devices, new materials, and a host of other things. So when you see the phrase technology start-up in this book, do not just think of the Internet and computer software companies, think of new businesses producing fuel cells, ceramic composites, new drugs, heart valves, and a variety of other things that are the embodiment of knowledge as a way to meet customer needs. Therefore, this is not just a book about how to create successful Internet or software companies; it is also a book about how to create successful companies in biotechnology, medical devices, materials, manufacturing components, and other industries that are reliant on new technology.

How This Book is Different from Other Books

This book is different from most books on entrepreneurship in three important ways. First, the book focuses on what matters the most for successful entrepreneurship—picking a good opportunity for starting a new business—rather than what most people write about—the attributes of successful entrepreneurs. Why is this latter approach a problem? Because of what academic research has shown about entrepreneurship. Despite decades of effort to identify the special features of successful entrepreneurs, there really are none. Anyone can become a successful entrepreneur. You do not need special psychological characteristics or attitudes. Take the example of Bill Gates. He is not a billion times more successful than the average entrepreneur who founds a restaurant because he has a billion times larger endowment of special psychological traits and attitudes than the average entrepreneur. Instead, Bill Gates is more successful because the creation of the DOS operating system—the technology on which he built Microsoft—created a superb opportunity for the creation of a new business. It was much more valuable than the opportunity for any of the retail or restaurant businesses that the average entrepreneur starts.

I do not mean to imply that entrepreneurial attitudes and talent do not help entrepreneurs. Certainly having better entrepreneurial talent and attitudes than other people helps entrepreneurs to perform better, all other things being equal. However, we live in a world where all other things are not equal, and what accounts for the vast majority of entrepreneurial success is the business opportunity that a person chooses to pursue. Academic research on entrepreneurship has shown that the effect of business opportunities on the performance of new ventures is so large that it swamps the effect of entrepreneurs' characteristics. While it wouldn't hurt to be a good entrepreneur no matter what business you start, what really matters is picking the right business for a start-up.

To put this in plain English, even at the risk of putting too fine a point on it, if you start a biotechnology firm, your chances of success are much greater than if you start a restaurant. The difference between a biotechnology firm and a restaurant is so great that the differences between individual entrepreneurs exert little more than a rounding error on the performance of the ventures.

If what separates successful entrepreneurs from everyone else is an understanding of how to pick the right opportunities for starting new companies, then what a good book on entrepreneurship should do is tell readers how to pick the right opportunities. Unfortunately, that isn't what most books do. This book differs from almost all other entrepreneurship books because it sets aside the discussion of the things that make some people better entrepreneurs than others and focuses attention on the characteristics of great opportunities for new businesses.

This book also is also different from most books on entrepreneurship, which focus on *how* to get a new company started rather than on what kind of business is a good one to start. While books on "how to start a business" are fine for answering questions like "how to incorporate a company" or "how to fill out tax form," they do nothing to help entrepreneurs to start successful companies. Unfortunately for entrepreneurs, there is no answer to the "how-to" question that is a secret to success. So there is no way to follow the recommendations of any of these how-to books to increase the chances of being a successful technology entrepreneur.

The "how-to-get-started books" miss the point of what would-be entrepreneurs need. As I said when I began this introduction, most people do not have a problem getting started in business; they have a harder time figuring out the right business to start. So what you need is a book that tells you how to pick a business opportunity that will make you successful, not how to get started in business. This book will help you to identify an opportunity for your new business and define your business concept.

Moreover, the book takes the idea of explaining how to pick the right business opportunity seriously by developing a framework of rules for success that are based on academic research which shows the things that make new companies successful. The book uses this framework to identify specific tools for identifying your business opportunity and developing your business concept that you can use to enhance the performance of your new company—such things as tools for the evaluation of customer needs for new products, tools for measuring adoption and diffusion patterns, tools for financing new companies, and tools for protecting a new venture's intellectual property. By bringing these tools together in one place and translating them from academic-speak into plain English, this book provides you with an understanding of how to create a successful new technology company.

This book additionally focuses on explaining how to identify a business concept that can support the development of a successful technology-based business. This is important because the performance of technology-based businesses—businesses such as the Internet, pollution abatement chemicals, high-temperature ceramics, fuel cells, and so on—depend on a variety of factors that are not present or are of relatively little importance in businesses not based on technology. The important factors in technology-based businesses, which are discussed in later chapters, include such things as intellectual property, increasing returns, dominant designs, diffusion, and S-curves. By explaining how to harness the factors that influence the performance of businesses in high-technology industries, this book provides you with the tools to create successful companies in these industries. Understanding and applying these tools helps you, as a high-technology entrepreneur, because the application of many concepts from low-technology business settings to high technology industries fails to help most entrepreneurs to be successful and, in some cases, even hinders their performance.

Why is this book's focus on the factors that matter to high-technology entrepreneurship unique? Given the fact that technology-based businesses are, on average, the most successful new businesses, you would think that many authors would focus their attention on these kinds of businesses. However, almost all existing books in the market discuss entrepreneurship in general, without considering the special nature of high technology. As a result, there really are no good guides available to explain to people the keys to success with high-technology enterprises. This book fills this void. It explains how the special characteristics of high technology influence what needs to be done to be successful with new technology-based businesses.

What This Book Does Not Do

Having said what this book does, it is only fair to tell you what it doesn't do. This book doesn't deal with the process of starting a company once you have identified your valuable opportunity. It doesn't deal with things like how to write a business plan or how to raise money or how to create a venture team or how to hire employees. There are many books out there that can explain these things to you. While it certainly wouldn't hurt to read these other books, the information contained in them is not a substitute for what is contained here. No matter what you do after you have identified a business opportunity, it is good to have selected a valuable one. And the lessons contained here will help you to do just that.

Who Should Read this Book and When Should They Read It?

You should read this book if you are thinking of starting a business. Ideally, you should read this book when you are first deciding what type of business you are going to start. Because this book focuses on identifying the fertile ground for your new business—what opportunity you should pursue and how you should pursue it—it is designed to help you conduct a feasibility analysis of your business opportunity. The frameworks described in the following pages, along with the recommendations for "dos" and "don'ts" and the questions to ask yourself are designed to help you to think about the business ideas that you come up with. Are they good for starting a new business? Will your venture be planted in fertile ground? Or will it be planted in arid soil that will make it very hard for you to succeed even if you are a great entrepreneur?

Moreover, you have probably thought of three or four ideas for a new business and you don't know which one to pursue. The discussion in the pages that follow will help you to figure out which of these opportunities is the best. After all, you are only going to be able to pursue one of your business ideas at a time. So you might as well pursue the best one first.

Even if you do not want to be the next Bill Gates, building the next big thing, taking your company public and becoming fabulously wealthy, this book will still be valuable to you. It is still easier to have a nice, comfortable business if you find fertile ground and pursue an opportunity that tends to favor start-up companies.

The Sources of Knowledge Underlying the Book

Because I have said that this book uses academic research to create a framework for understanding how to create successful technology-based new companies, it is only fair for me to tell you the source of information underlying this book. The book has two specific sources of information. Some parts of the framework and evidence presented here are based on my own primary research. Other parts are based on the research of other academics. Regardless of the source, this book compiles, combines, and translates into plain English, material that is otherwise available only in a variety of different academic articles and books. As a result, you will find all of the key concepts that you need to understand to be a successful technology entrepreneur summarized and explained in one place, presented in a clear and straightforward manner.

The Key Lessons

Successful technology entrepreneurs approach entrepreneurship differently from other entrepreneurs, not because they are smarter than or different from other people, but because they have learned how to identify valuable opportunities for new technology companies. This book presents ten rules for entrepreneurs to follow to develop a business concept that will provide the basis for a successful high-technology company. Each of these rules is explained in a different chapter of the book. The rules are

1. Select the right industry

2. Identify valuable opportunities

3. Manage technological transitions

4. Identify and satisfy real market needs

5. Understand customer adoption

6. Exploit established company weaknesses

7. Manage intellectual property

8. Create barriers to imitation

9. Choose the right organizational form

10. Manage risk and uncertainty

An Overview of the Chapters

The first rule of technology entrepreneurship explained in this book is to select the right industry in which to found a new firm. Some industries are simply better than other industries for the creation of new companies. For instance, fully one-fourth of all the companies listed on Inc magazine's list of the 500 fastest growing private companies since 1982 have been software firms. Moreover, the proportion of start-ups in an industry that experience an initial public offering or are listed in the *Inc* 500 varies by a factor of over 800 times between some of the more favorable industries and some of the less favorable ones. Chapter 1 identifies the industries that are favorable for founding new firms and explains why those industries are more favorable to new firms than other industries. Specifically, the chapter examines five different dimensions of industry differences that influence the performance of new firms: knowledge conditions, demand conditions, industry life cycles, the presence or absence of a dominant design, and industry structure.

The second rule of technology entrepreneurship is to identify valuable opportunities. One of the ironies of entrepreneurship is that, despite the motivation of the world's entrepreneurs, we do not really need many new businesses. Established businesses are already meeting most market needs quite effectively because, in the absence of some sort of external change, someone will have figured out already how to satisfy the needs of potential customers. Therefore, to be a successful technology entrepreneur, you have to find an external change that creates an opportunity for a new business. Chapter 2 explains why opportunities for new technology companies exist and what the sources of those opportunities are. In general, three sources of change—new technology, political and regulatory shifts, and social and demographic movements—open up opportunities. The chapter also discusses the types of innovations that generate entrepreneurial opportunities, as well as the place within and outside the value chain where those innovations tend to occur. Furthermore, the chapter explains why and how some people and not others identify those opportunities.

The third rule of technology entrepreneurship is to manage technological transitions. Entrepreneurial success is enhanced by starting a firm to transition from one technological paradigm to another because change in a technological paradigm undermines the advantage of established firms. For example, few entrepreneurs have ever been able to start new firms that challenge Kodak's position in traditional film, but the shift to digital camera technology made it possible for many entrepreneurs to enter and compete with Kodak. Chapter 3 explains how you can manage technological transitions to become successful. The chapter explains

- Why technologies follow evolutionary patterns of change that open up discrete points of transition between technological paradigms that are valuable to entrepreneurs.

- How you can forecast the S-shaped pattern of technological development and use this pattern to manage when and how to enter industries.

- How dominant designs influence competition by entrepreneurial ventures.

- How you can exploit technical standards to enhance the success of your new business.

- What you should do differently to be successful in increasing returns businesses, which are common in high technology.

The fourth rule of technology entrepreneurship is to identify and satisfy a real market need. To be successful, you must introduce a new product or service that offers an economical solution to an unsatisfied customer need or that satisfies a customer need better than existing alternatives. Chapter 4 explains how successful entrepreneurs go about identifying customer needs for high technology products and services in ways that go beyond the traditional market research methods of surveys and focus groups. The chapter provides insight into why and how the advantages of successful new firms lie in product development rather than in manufacturing or marketing. Finally, the chapter explains how successful technology entrepreneurs identify the key decision makers in purchasing decisions, as well as how these entrepreneurs price their new products and services to make them attractive to these decision makers.

The fifth rule of technology entrepreneurship is to understand customer adoption and market dynamics. Contrary to the popular conception that evaluating markets is as simple as looking for large markets, evaluating markets for new technology products and services is relatively complicated. In particular, it requires successful entrepreneurs to take a dynamic approach that forecasts the adoption patterns for new technology products and services and explains how markets for these products and services evolve. Chapter 5 explains why new companies have to focus their new product or service development efforts on particular market segments, but why choosing where to focus effort is hard to do. The chapter also explains how successful entrepreneurs evaluate the customer and their reasons to buy as a way to determine where to focus their efforts. Furthermore, the chapter discusses the evolution of markets for new technology products and services, particularly the dynamics of technology diffusion and substitution.

The sixth rule of technology entrepreneurship is to exploit established company weaknesses. Most of the time, established companies succeed when they compete with new firms because of the wealth of advantages in marketing and manufacturing that they have. However, established firms have several weaknesses that hinder their efforts to exploit technological opportunities that new firms can exploit. Chapter 6 identifies what you should do to compete successfully with established firms in high-technology settings. For instance, the chapter explains why you should pursue uncertain, disruptive technologies that demand new architectures, first focusing on niche customers in small market segments, and then expanding up market. The chapter also explains why you should focus on technologies that cannibalize established firms' investments, make established firm capabilities obsolete, and impose large exit costs on firms using the old technology.

The seventh rule of technology entrepreneurship is to manage intellectual property effectively. Introducing a product or service that meets a market need is a necessary, but not sufficient condition to profit from innovation. You must also protect your innovation against imitation. Chapter 7 discusses basic ideas behind appropriating the returns to innovation, focusing on the choice between secrecy and patenting.

The eighth rule of technology entrepreneurship is to create barriers to imitation. Chapter 8 examines how you can create barriers to imitation by controlling resources, establishing a reputation, creating a first mover advantage, exploiting the learning curve, and making use of complementary assets in manufacturing, marketing and distribution.

The ninth rule of technology entrepreneurship is to choose the right organizational form. Chapter 9 explains when you are best off owning the various parts of the value chain, such as product development, manufacturing, and distribution, and when you are best off using market-based mechanisms, such as licensing, franchising, and strategic alliances, to control them.

The tenth rule of technology entrepreneurship is to manage risk and uncertainty effectively. Chapter 10 describes the tools and techniques that successful entrepreneurs use to reduce, reallocate, and manage risk. The chapter also discusses the use of real options and scenario analysis, as well as behavioral techniques for convincing others to bear risk, such as escalation of commitment, bringing together different parties at the same time, and closing skills.

The conclusion of the book returns to the theme introduced in the first chapter about the importance of understanding how to identify valuable opportunities for the creation of new technology companies. Specifically, it summarizes the key actions that you should take to come up with an opportunity that will support, and even foster, the creation of a new high-technology company.

The next chapter explores the first key lesson in starting a successful new high-technology company: picking the right industry.

1

SELECTING THE RIGHT INDUSTRY

While entrepreneurs like to think of themselves as being able to over-come all of the obstacles that life puts in front of them, being a suc-cessful technology entrepreneur is really more about playing the odds successfully. While you certainly need to temper playing the odds with playing to your strength, and make sure that you do not pursue a venture in an industry that you know nothing about, you need to keep in mind that your success depends a great deal on selecting the right industry in which to launch a new firm. Some industries oper-ate through dynamics of creative destruction, and, as a result, entre-preneurs tend to perform very well. In these industries, entrepre-neurs enter with new firms, challenge established firms on the basis of new ideas, disrupt the old ways of production, organization, and distribution and replace the old firms. Examples of industries in which this process of creative destruction appears to operate and entrepreneurs tend to do very well are chemical processes, comput-er disk drives, machine tools and lighting.[1]

Other industries operate through dynamics of creative accumulation and entrepreneurs tend to perform very poorly. In these industries, entrepreneurs enter and challenge established firms on the basis of their new ideas. However, established firms defend their old ways of production, organization, and distribution, and the new firms tend to fail. Examples of industries in which this process of creative accumulation tends to be found are organic chemicals, telecommunications, and electronics.[2]

This chapter focuses on identifying the attributes that make an industry favorable to new firms. The first section provides empirical evidence of the differences in the favorability of different industries to new firms. The subsequent sections each review different dimensions of industry differences that influence the performance of new firms: knowledge conditions, demand conditions, industry life cycles, and industry structure.

Looking at the Evidence

If you are thinking of starting a new technology company, you can and should examine how favorable different industries are to new firms. A former PhD student of mine, Jon Eckhardt, who is now on the faculty at the University of Wisconsin, compared the proportion of startups in different industries that made the *Inc* 500, the magazine's list of the fastest growing young private companies. Looking from 1982 to 2000, Jon found very high levels of variation in this measure (see Table 1.1).[3] For instance, Jon's data show that the odds of starting a biotechnology company that made the *Inc* 500 were 265 times higher than the odds of starting a restaurant that made the *Inc* 500 and that the odds of starting a computer software company that made the list was 823 times higher than the odds of starting a hotel that made the list. In short, an average entrepreneur starting an average new firm will be more likely to create a high-growth private company or a newly public company in some industries than in others.

TABLE 1.1 **Percent of New Firms in Selected Industries That Have Become _Inc 500_ Firms.**

Industry	Percent of Start-ups
Pulp mills	18.2
Computer and office equipment	4.2
Guided missiles, space vehicles, parts	3.3
Nonferrous rolling and drawing	2.4
Railroad car rental	2.2
Measuring and controlling devices	2.0
Paper mills	2.0
Search and navigation equipment	1.9
Communications equipment	1.9
Drugs	1.8
Medical instruments and supplies	1.8
Luggage	1.7
Footwear, except rubber	1.5
Security and commodity exchanges	1.4
Steam and air-conditioning supply	1.2
General industrial machinery	1.2
Photographic equipment and supplies	1.1
Manifold business forms	1.1
Household appliances	1.0
Electrical industrial apparatus	1.0
Legal services	0.008
Eating and drinking places	0.007
Carpentry and floor work contractors	0.006
Real estate operators	0.006
Hotels and motels	0.005
Painting and paper hanging contractors	0.005
Retail bakeries	0.005
Grocery stores	0.005
Used merchandise stores	0.004
Automotive repair shops	0.004
Beauty shops	0.004
Residential care	0.004
Video tape rental	0.004

Stop! Don't Do It!

1. Don't start a business without investigating how favorable the industry is to new firms.
2. Don't fight the odds. Don't start a business in an industry that is unfavorable to start-ups.

So how do we explain these data patterns? Unless most of the talented entrepreneurs are drawn to some industries (e.g., biotechnology) and not others (e.g., hotels), some industries are just better for starting new firms than others. This, of course, means that you need to understand the characteristics of industries that make some of them better for starting firms than others if you want to increase your chances of success. Research has shown that four different dimensions matter: knowledge conditions, demand conditions, industry life cycles, and industry structure.

Knowledge Conditions

Certain industries are more favorable to new firms than other industries because of the knowledge conditions underlying the industry. Why? Because some knowledge conditions are easier for new firms to manage, while others require the expertise of established firms.

One aspect of knowledge conditions is the level of complexity of the production process. Production in some industries is more complex than production in other industries. For example, the production process in the aerospace industry is more complex than in the paper bag manufacturing business because the number of factors that need to be incorporated into the production process, the level of precision involved in making the products, and the sophistication of the required knowledge are all higher in aerospace than in paper bag manufacturing.

Industries that involve very complex production processes tend to be unfavorable to new firms. Complex production processes require sophisticated organization structures to coordinate the activities of people engaged in a wide variety of activities. These sophisticated organization structures are easier to implement in established firms that have more specialized labor, larger management teams, and routines for the management of complex operations. Moreover, the knowledge of how to undertake complex activities is often developed through learning by doing over time. Therefore, new firms often have less knowledge of such activities than established companies.

Another aspect of knowledge conditions is the amount of new knowledge creation that is required to generate the industry's products and services. For instance, the pharmaceutical industry relies very heavily on the creation of new knowledge to produce its products and services. Absent basic scientific research, it would be difficult for pharmaceutical researchers to create new drugs. In contrast, the dry cleaning industry does not rely very much on basic scientific research to create its products and services. In fact, dry cleaning services can be offered without very much new knowledge creation at all.

Industries that rely greatly on new knowledge creation, as measured by the proportion of their sales that they devote to research and development (R&D), are less favorable to new firms. New firms perform worse in more knowledge intensive industries because they do not have the internal cash flow to invest in basic research—a situation that creates a larger handicap in R&D intensive industries than in other industries. Moreover, basic research is often very uncertain and can result in the creation of new products or services in very different lines of businesses than those for which it was originally intended. Large, established organizations with economies of scope are more likely to benefit from investing in this type of uncertain research and development than small, new firms. This does not mean you can't start a successful new company in an R&D intensive industry; many founders of biotechnology companies have done just that. It only means that the R&D intensity is making it harder for you to succeed.

Another dimension of knowledge conditions in an industry that affects the performance of start-ups concerns the codification (the writing down) of knowledge. In some industries, the knowledge necessary to undertake the development of new products and services is readily available in written form. For instance, there are numerous books and articles on computer networking. However, in other industries, this knowledge lies in the heads of experienced personnel who know how to undertake that activity effectively, but who cannot specify in written form the causal mechanisms that lead to performance. Some aspects of circuit design, for example, are known to only a handful of individuals.

Codification of knowledge enhances the performance of new firms because codified knowledge is more easily available to entrepreneurs than is tacit (residing in the heads of a few) knowledge. Because codified knowledge is written down, it is available to entrepreneurs who do not have direct operating experience in the industry. In contrast, tacit knowledge is only available to entrepreneurs with direct operating experience in the industry or who hire those with direct operating experience. As a result, learning curves are less proprietary in industries in which knowledge is codified, allowing new firms to more easily learn what predecessors have learned about an industry and catch up in terms of performance.

Yet another important dimension of knowledge conditions concerns where the innovation that makes new products and services possible is developed. In some industries, such as semiconductors, innovation occurs within the industry itself (sometimes referred to as the "value chain"). Firms and their customers and suppliers generate most innovations. In other industries, such as superconductors, extra-value chain organizations, such as universities, produce much more of the innovation than firms within the value chain.

New firms perform best in industries in which extra-value chain entities produce most of the innovation. Universities and public research institutions are less concerned than firms about keeping valuable knowledge from leaking out to others. In fact, senior managers at companies like Intel take explicit actions, such as having employees sign noncompete agreements and restricting access to research laboratories, to keep valuable knowledge within the organization. In contrast, senior administrators at universities, like MIT, take explicit actions, such as encouraging corporate tours of laboratories and sharing papers at industrywide meetings, to encourage knowledge transfer out of the organization. Because new firms cannot create much of the knowledge necessary to innovate, industries in which public sector organizations conduct much of the knowledge creation, and knowledge spillovers are relatively large, are those in which new firms perform the best.[4]

Industries also differ in the distribution in proportion of value added that comes from manufacturing and marketing activities, as opposed to product development and innovation. In some industries, such as automobiles, much of the value added comes from manufacturing and marketing, rather than from product development. In other industries, such as software, manufacturing and marketing account for a much smaller proportion of value added, with some companies having virtually no manufacturing or distribution assets.

New firms tend to perform poorly in industries in which manufacturing and marketing account for most of the value added. When firms create new products and services, they often need manufacturing and marketing assets to exploit those innovations. As a result, established firms figure out how to market and manufacture effectively and make those activities routine. New firms are at a disadvantage when competing with established firms because they have not yet figured out how to make these activities routine. So their manufacturing and marketing are often quite inefficient.

Stop! Don't Do It!

1. Don't ignore the knowledge conditions of the industry you are thinking of entering.
2. Don't start a company in an industry in which knowledge conditions are unfavorable to new firms.

Moreover, manufacturing and marketing assets are often very expensive—think about the cost of creating an automobile plant—and are difficult to outsource. Manufacturing operations often need specialized assets, such as expensive machines designed to produce specific products, making it very difficult to find someone willing to provide those assets on a contractual basis. As a result, established firms tend to own the necessary manufacturing and marketing assets, making it difficult for new firms to get access to equivalent marketing and manufacturing assets at the time of founding, which handicaps them in their efforts to compete with established firms. Thus, new firms tend to perform more poorly in industries such as automobiles, where the manufacturing and marketing assets are important, than they do in industries such as computer software, where these assets are less important.

Demand Conditions

Another important dimension of industry is called "demand conditions" and refers to the nature of customer preferences. For instance, more consumers may feel they need a new computer that is faster and has more memory than they need, say, a device that locates the "studs" in a house's walls. Three aspects of demand conditions in an industry are important for entrepreneurs to understand: the magnitude of customer demand for products or services, the rate growth of that demand, and the heterogeneity of that demand across customer segments.

These aspects of demand conditions are important for entrepreneurs because they influence the performance of new firms. The magnitude of customer demand has a positive effect on new firm performance, leading new firms to perform better in larger markets. For example, new biotechnology firms tend to perform better when developing cures to major medical problems than when they pursue the development of orphan drugs. Why? New firms must incur a fixed cost to organize and produce a product to meet demand in an industry. As a result, the new firm's average cost of meeting demand is smaller in a larger market than in a smaller market. Because established firms have already incurred the fixed cost of organizing, they can meet demand at marginal cost, which is lower than average cost. The cost gap between new and established firm efforts to meet demand is smaller in larger markets than in smaller ones, making larger markets more favorable to new companies than smaller markets. Most venture capitalists understand this logic, which is why they often focus their attention on backing those start-ups pursuing the largest markets.

The performance of new firms is also higher in rapidly growing markets than in slowly growing markets. Why? Because the more rapidly a market grows, the less a new firm needs to serve the customers of existing firms.[5] Serving new customers, rather than the customers of existing firms, is advantageous because established companies compete more fiercely to protect their existing customers than they do to gain new customers, making the level of competition for new firms lower in rapidly growing industries.

Finally, the degree of segmentation of the market affects the favorability of an industry to new firms. Market segmentation refers to the degree to which the customer base of an industry wants different features in the products or services it demands. Some industries are composed of customers with very different combinations of preferences than others. That is, some markets are more segmented than others. Clothing is a good example of a highly segmented industry. Not only are there differences between men's, women's, and children's fashions, but there are large differences in quality, color, and other preferences. In contrast, water purification is an industry with very little segmentation. Basically, everyone wants clean water, and there is limited variation in preferences across customers in the features of purified water.

New firms benefit from segmented markets. Given the small scale at which most new firms are founded, they cannot service the entire market immediately upon entry. Segmented markets provide an opportunity for new firms to enter with small-scale production and serve the underserved niches. Usually, new firms face less competition from established firms when they enter markets in this way. Because established firms focus on their mainstream customers, they often retaliate when new firms enter unsegmented markets. In these markets, new firms are targeting their main customers. In contrast, when new firms enter underserved niches, established firms do not feel that their customer base is under attack and are more likely accommodate entry. Take, for example, the efforts by Nucor to enter the steel industry. Because Nucor initially targeted the segment of the steel market where the profit margins were the slimmest, the major steel makers accommodated its entry. Had Nucor first entered the highest margin segment of the market first, the major steel makers would likely have retaliated.

Stop! Don't Do It!

1. Don't start a business is a small market; you can just as easily start one in a large market.
2. Don't start a business in a slow growth market; your competitors will respond viciously.
3. Don't start a business in an unsegmented market; the competition from established firms will kill your business.

Industry Life Cycles

The stage of an industry in its life cycle is another dimension of industry that affects the performance of new firms. Industries, like people and new products, are born, grow, mature, and die out. This life cycle impacts the performance of new firms because new firms tend to perform better when industries are first born, or are young and growing, than when they are mature or are dying out.[6] There are several reasons why. Customer adoption of new products and services is typically normally distributed. As is shown in chapter 6, a few customers are willing to be the initial adopters of new technology products and services, but most people wait until new technology products and services have been around a while before adopting. Similarly, a small number of people tend to be the late adopters of new technology products and services because they are laggards in their view of new products in general. The majority of adopters fall somewhere in the middle, adopting neither early nor late.[7]

Because the number of people who adopt early and late is smaller than the number of people who adopt in the middle, markets grow slowly at first, accelerate, and then slow back down. The small number of people adopting initially leads to slow market growth. The increased number of people adopting in the middle period leads to an acceleration in market growth. Then the decreased number of people adopting in later periods leads to a deceleration in market growth.

New firms perform better in young markets than in old ones because it is easier for new firms to attract customers when demand growth is highest. Under these conditions, they face the least severe competition from established firms. As an example, think of the cell phone business. In the early growth phase of the market, new firms had a relatively easy time attracting customers. After all, when the demand for cell phones was growing at double digits, there were enough customers for everyone. However, as the industry began to mature and growth slowed, established firms began to compete more heavily for their customers, making it harder for new firms to attract them.

In young industries, new firms face fewer competitors. At the beginning of an industry, no companies yet exist to meet customer demand for the new industry's products and services. Over time, firms enter to meet demand, generating competition to attract the same customers. Moreover, when industries mature, firms exit more slowly than the reduction of demand indicates that they should. This exit stickiness means that mature industries are often very competitive, with established firms fighting very hard to maintain their market position against persistent demand reductions across all suppliers. As a result, new firms tend to perform better when industries are young than when they are old.

As an example, think about the personal computer business. In the beginning, there were no firms providing this product, but as the products became more established, many firms entered this market space. This entry caused fierce competition among firms in the industry, drove down prices, and has made it more and more difficult for new firms to compete.

Most products and services involve a learning curve. The learning curve allows firms to use their experience operating in an industry to improve their efforts to meet customer demand. Such things as manufacturing, selling, and responding to customer complaints all involve learning by doing, which favors established firms. New firms, by definition, lack the operating experience that established firms have, and so have learning curve disadvantages vis-à-vis established firms. Because experience is gained over time through operating activity, the magnitude of the learning curve disadvantage is smallest when the industry is young and largest when the industry is old. Thus, new firms are more disadvantaged in older industries.

Initially, many industries face competing designs for products. However, as industries mature, they evolve toward the adoption of a dominant design or technical standard that is common to all products or services in an industry. Take, for instance, the production of nuts and bolts. While it may seem hard to believe, 150 years ago, nuts and bolts were not interchangeable. They were all manufactured by different companies to different designs. Today, nuts and bolts manufactured adhere to a common standard that makes them interchangeable.

The tendency of industries to converge on a dominant design or technical standard is important to a new firm's performance because new firms tend to perform much better before the adoption of a dominant design or technical standard than after it. Prior to the adoption of a dominant design or technical standard, entrepreneurs are not constrained in the designs that they can employ. Once a dominant design has been adopted, however, entrepreneurs are constrained to those designs that are consistent with the dominant standard. Because established firms have greater experience working with an established design than new firms do, new firms are disadvantaged once a dominant design emerges in an industry.[8]

Moreover, the nature of competition changes after a dominant design has emerged in an industry. Because designs tend to become standardized, what separates one company from another after a dominant design emerges changes from the design itself to the production process. After a dominant design or technical standard has emerged, competition shifts to production efficiency. The experience and size of established companies allows them to produce the standard design more efficiently than new firms and hinders new firm performance once the dominant design or technical standard has emerged.[9]

Stop! Don't Do It!

1. Don't wait until a business is mature to enter.
2. Don't wait until after a dominant design has emerged to start your firm.

Industry Structure

A final dimension of industry that is important to the performance of new firms is industry structure. The structure of the industry refers to the nature of barriers to entry and competitive dynamics in the industry. Four characteristics of industry structure are particularly important to the performance of new firms in the industry: capital intensity, advertising intensity, concentration, and average firm size.

Capital intensity measures the importance of capital as opposed to labor in the production process. Some industries, such as aerospace, involve a great deal of capital and relatively little labor. Other industries, such as textiles, involve relatively little capital and a great deal of labor.

New firms perform better in labor intensive industries (ones where work matters more than money) than in capital intensive ones.[10] Why? At the time that they are founded, new firms lack cash flow from existing operations. Yet new firms need to expend capital to establish the organization and create production and distribution assets. Because new firms must expend capital before they have cash flow from operations, they must obtain capital from external capital markets. Capital obtained from financial markets is more expensive than internally generated capital. Investors demand a premium for bearing the risk that comes from the gap of information between investors and entrepreneurs. The magnitude of this premium is related to the size of the capital requirement necessary to create the business. The larger the capital requirement, the greater the disadvantage faced by new firms in the industry.

New firms are disadvantaged relative to established firms in more advertising intensive industries. Advertising is a mechanism through which companies develop the reputations that help them sell their products and services. To build a brand name reputation through advertising, two conditions need to be met. First, the advertising has to be repeated over time. The capacities of human beings are such that they can only absorb so much information at a time. Therefore, it takes time for new firms to build their brand names, during which time they have lesser reputations than existing firms. Second, economies of scale exist in advertising. The cost of advertising is largely fixed, regardless of the number of units of a product sold. As a result, the cost per unit of advertising decreases with the volume of sales. New firms tend to produce fewer units than established firms because they begin operations at a small scale, making their per unit advertising costs higher than those of established firms.[11] Of course, this advertising disadvantage is more problematic the more important advertising is for an industry, making new firms less competitive with established firms in more advertising intensive industries than in less advertising intensive ones.

New firms are disadvantaged relative to established firms in more concentrated industries.[12] Concentration is a measure of the market share that is held by the largest companies in an industry. For instance, in some industries, such as pharmaceuticals (think of how few drugs you use are made by firms other than the big pharmaceutical companies like Merck, Pfizer, and Eli Lilly), the largest companies account for almost all of the market. In contrast, in more fragmented industries, like dry cleaning, virtually no firm has even 1 percent of the total market.

New firms perform relatively poorly in concentrated industries because industry concentration provides large, established firms with market power. In concentrated industries, such as telecommunications firms offering local phone service, established firms have the resources to keep new firms from establishing a beachhead in the industry. As a result, they use their monopoly or oligopoly profits to deter entry. Moreover, entry can be deterred more easily in concentrated industries than in fragmented industries for two reasons. First, in fragmented industries, there are small, vulnerable firms that can be challenged more successfully than the large, powerful firms that are the only competitors in concentrated industries. Second, in concentrated industries, established firms can collude to keep other firms from entering. For instance, they can collectively cut prices when a new entrant comes into the industry until that entrant is driven out of business and then raise prices again. Because collusion only works if all of the colluders participate, it is much easier to pull off when there are few players in an industry than when there are many.

New firms perform better in industries in which the average size of firms is small.[13] New firms tend to begin small as a way to minimize the risk of entrepreneurial miscalculation. That is, if entrepreneurs begin small, they have a lower downside loss if they are incorrect. In industries in which most firms are small, starting a new firm at a small scale does not create much of a disadvantage relative to the established firms in the industry.[14] In contrast, in industries where the average firm size is large, starting small creates a number of disadvantages, such as the inability to purchase in volume and higher average manufacturing and distribution costs due to the absence of economies of scale. As an example, think of the difference between Web site developers and steel mills. Because the average Web site developer is small, a new small Web site developer is able to operate at almost the same scale, if not the same scale, as the established players. However, the average steel mill is quite large. So, if a new steel mill is started small, it is initially at a great disadvantage relative to the established firms with which it needs to compete.

Stop! Don't Do It!

1. Don't start a business in a capital intensive industry.
2. Don't start a business in an advertising intensive industry.
3. Don't start a business in an industry in which the average sized firms are large.
4. Don't start a business in a concentrated market.

Questions to Ask Yourself

1. Is the industry that I am planning to enter a good one for start-ing a new company?

2. Are the knowledge conditions in the industry favorable to a start-up?

3. Are demand conditions in the industry favorable to a start-up?

4. Is the industry at the right stage of the life cycle for a start-up?

5. Is the industry structure favorable for a start-up?

Summary

This chapter explained that the first rule for success as a technology entrepreneur lies in choosing the right industry. The performance of new firms varies significantly across industries, and can influence by up to a factor of 1,000, the probability that an entrepreneur will establish an *Inc* 500 firm or will take a firm public. Researchers have identified four dimensions of industry that affect the relative performance of new firms: knowledge conditions, demand conditions, stage of the industry life cycle, and market structure. You can benefit from understanding the specific effects that each of these dimensions of industry has on the performance of new firms.

Industry knowledge conditions are composed of five factors that affect the relative performance of new firms in an industry. New firms perform poorly in industries in which the production process is complex, the amount of new knowledge created in an industry is high, knowledge is not well codified, the locus of innovation resides within the value chain, and complementary assets in marketing and manufacturing are important.

Industry demand conditions are composed of three factors that affect the performance of new firms in an industry. In industries in which markets are large, growing quickly, and heavily segmented, new firms perform well.

The industry life cycle also affects the relative performance of new firms in an industry. New firms perform better when industries are younger than they do when industries are older. New firms also perform better when a dominant design does not exist in an industry than when a dominant design does exist in an industry.

Four aspects of industry structure affect the performance of new firms in an industry. New firms perform poorly in industries that are capital intensive, advertising intensive, concentrated, and have large firms.

Now that you understand rule number one of technology entrepreneurship, selecting the right industry, we now turn to rule number two, identifying valuable opportunities, which is the subject of the next chapter.

2

IDENTIFYING VALUABLE OPPORTUNITIES

Most of the time, the world does not need new businesses because established firms are meeting customer needs effectively. As a result, there is no opportunity for entrepreneurs to create successful new companies. Sadly, many entrepreneurs do not realize this, and create new businesses in the absence of business opportunities. These new businesses fail in a short amount of time.

To be successful, you need to start your new business in response to an opportunity to create a new product or service that meets customer needs that have not been satisfied adequately, or that satisfies customer needs in a much better way than established companies satisfy them. So, where do these opportunities come from? What form do they take? How do successful entrepreneurs match opportunities to innovation? How do successful entrepreneurs identify these opportunities? This chapter answers these questions.

Sources of Opportunities

Entrepreneurial opportunities are situations in which a person has a chance to introduce a product that generates more revenues than it costs to produce. These situations exist when customers' needs are not being satisfied or when it is possible to satisfy those needs in a better way than is currently being done. So, why do these opportunities exist? After all, if the opportunities are valuable, then why hasn't someone else exploited them already?

One reason why is that some type of change has just occurred to open up an opportunity to do something new or do something in a better way.[1] Take, for example, the opportunity to record music on compact disks. This opportunity did not exist until the invention of the laser made it possible.

The relationship between change and the creation of opportunity indicates that the first step in identifying a valuable opportunity is identifying the change that makes the opportunity possible. In general, four types of changes make opportunities for new businesses: changes in technology, changes in political and regulatory rules, changes in social and demographic factors, and changes in industry structure. Successful entrepreneurs understand how each of these sources generates a change that makes entrepreneurial opportunities possible.

Technological Change

As you might expect, technological change is one of the most important triggers of opportunities to start new high technology companies, largely because technological change allows people to do things that could not be done before or only could be done in a less efficient manner.[2] Take, for example, the invention of the computer software behind e-mail. This software made it possible to communicate in ways that are more efficient than the telephone, fax, or letters, and so opened up a valuable opportunity.

So, what attributes of technological change are associated with the creation of valuable opportunities for new businesses? The magnitude of the technological change is important. The larger the technological change, the greater the opportunity for new businesses to be created because larger magnitude changes affect more uses for technology, allowing the use of new technology in more things. Take, for instance, the creation of a new type of electrical circuit. If that new circuit is only 10 percent faster than an older one, it will replace the older circuit in only a small number of things. Only those products in which a 10 percent improvement would exceed the cost of change will use the new circuit. In contrast, if the new circuit is 500 percent faster than the older one, its benefits will exceed the cost of the change in a much larger range of things.

Then there is the generality of the change. Some technologies, like the laser, are general-purpose technologies. They lead to the creation of a wide range of new products. For instance, the laser made possible such new products as supermarket scanners, medical devices, and compact disk players. Because general-purpose technologies can be applied in a wide range of areas, they open up more opportunities for new products and services than single-purpose technologies.

There is also the commercial viability of the change. Some new technologies have a large magnitude effect, but do not directly result in much commercial benefit. For instance, the space shuttle is a very large change over alternatives for getting into space because it saves a huge amount of money over rockets that cannot be reused. However, the commercial benefits of the space shuttle are rather limited because there are only a few commercial applications to which it can be put.

Finally, there is the effect of the technological change on industry dynamics. One reason why technological change is often a major source of opportunity to start new businesses is that it alters how firms compete with one another. Take, for example, the effect of voice over Internet protocol in the telephone business. This technology has turned a capital intensive business into one that requires little capital. As a result, it creates opportunities for new firms, who are at a disadvantage in capital intensive industries.

Political and Regulatory Change

Another type of change that opens up opportunities for new businesses is political and regulatory change. This type of change creates opportunities because it is productivity enhancing. For instance, the deregulation of telecommunications allowed many new firms to form and introduce less expensive ways to transmit voice and data that benefited both businesses and consumers.[3]

In other cases, the opportunity that political and regulatory changes generate is not productive, but merely shifts value from one set of economic factors to another. For instance, a town ordinance that requires everyone in the town to use two grounding rods for electricity, even through one grounding rod is all that is necessary for safety, would create an opportunity for an entrepreneur to take wealth away from consumers. Because the grounding rod has no actual benefit, the ordinance creates an opportunity that is not productive, but rather is wealth shifting.

Why do political and regulatory changes enhance entrepreneurial opportunity? Deregulation creates opportunity because it allows more variance in ideas to be put forward by entrepreneurs who might have been barred from entry under a regulated regime. Deregulation also eliminates many of bureaucratic barriers and obstacles to creating new businesses. Many entrepreneurs do not create new businesses because the cost of such activity becomes too high under regulated regimes. When deregulation occurs, entrepreneurs see firm formation as profitable in ways that had not been profitable before.

Specific regulations also make possible activities that those regulations are designed to support by increasing demand for them. For instance, a regulation that mandates the use of car seats increases demand for them, and opens up opportunities to manufacture and sell car seats.

Some political and regulatory changes offer subsidies or other resources to support certain activities, cutting the costs of those activities and making them more common. For example, economist Maryann Feldman from the University of Toronto found that the U.S. government's procurement policies made it possible for new information technology companies to be formed in the Washington, D.C., region.[4] By taking advantage of the federal government's new rules for procuring IT services, many new companies were able to find a market for their services and get off the ground.

Social and Demographic Change

Another important category of change that generates entrepreneurial opportunities is social and demographic change. Social and demographic changes open up opportunities for new technology businesses by altering people's preferences and creating demand for things where demand had not existed before. For instance, the demographic shift of women into the workforce, and the corresponding increase in demand for speed in food preparation, created the opportunity to introduce many types of frozen food into the marketplace.

One important type of social and demographic change that creates opportunities is a social trend. For example, the opportunity to produce deodorant was the result of a social trend that led the majority of the population to believe that body odor was offensive. While there is actually no medical or health need for people to mask body odor, the development social trend to believe that body odor is offensive made it possible to create products that mask that odor.

Demographic trends are another important type of change that leads to the creation of entrepreneurial opportunities. For example, as birth rates decline and people live longer, the U.S. population is aging. This demographic trend makes it possible to introduce products and services for which sufficient demand did not exist 25 years ago, such as those in geriatric health care.

Yet another type of social or demographic change is a shift in perception or demand. Sometimes, people decide that they would like something different or perceive things in a new way. A good example of this type of change is the perception of the American flag after the events of September 11. The demand for the American flag increased dramatically, largely because of changes in the perceptions of the American public about what the flag symbolizes.

Some changes combine both social and technological factors. For instance, companies such as Net Nanny and Cyber Patrol have taken advantage of an opportunity to protect children against harmful Internet content. This opportunity came about both because of the technological development of the Internet and the social trend of children being home alone after school.

Changes in Industry Structure

Another type of change that is a source of entrepreneurial opportunities is change in industry structure. Sometimes, industry structure shifts because firms that supply other firms or major customers die or because firms merge or acquire each other. These types of shifts change the competitive dynamics in an industry and open up or close down niches that may provide opportunities for entrepreneurs. For instance, as the airline industry consolidated based on the hub and spoke design that major airlines use, opportunities for entrepreneurs

Stop! Don't Do It!

1. Don't start a business without first identifying the source of opportunity for it.

2. Don't start a business unless you understand how technological, political, regulatory, social, demographic, or industrial change created an opportunity for it.

to enter and create new airlines that fly point-to-point began to occur. The shift to the hub and spoke approach alone was not sufficient to create an opportunity for new firms to enter; it was the combination of the change in the air travel industry combined with firm exit that generated this business opportunity.

Forms of Opportunity: Beyond New Products or Services

The next step in the process of identifying valuable entrepreneurial opportunities is to understand the form that those opportunities take. While it is common to think of technological, political/regulatory, social/demographic, and industrial structure changes as opening up entrepreneurial opportunities by making it possible to introduce new products and services that had not previously existed, these changes also create opportunities by allowing older products and services to be produced with new production methods, using new raw materials, organized in new ways, or for sale in new markets.[5]

The invention of the laser and the creation of the compact disk is an example of a change making a new product or service possible. Jeff Bezos's founding of Amazon.com to sell books, a very old product, on the Internet, is an example of a change making possible new methods of organizing a firm. The business of freezing and canning meat and selling it in other countries is an example of a way to take an old product and find a new market for that product. The substitution of ceramic composites for metals in the production of vehicles is an example of the use of new materials to create an existing product in new ways. Finally, continuous strip production is an example of a new production process used by steel minimills to make an existing product, steel, through a different production process from the traditional continuous casting approach.

Why do the different forms opportunities take matter for entrepreneurs? The most important answer is that very often technology entrepreneurs think in terms of creating new products and services even through producing old products and services through new ways of organizing, using new raw materials, new production processes, and targeting to new markets are actually better approaches to follow. As you will explore in greater detail in chapters 7 and 8, success requires entrepreneurs to develop products and services that competitors will not immediately imitate. Researchers have demonstrated that simply entering a new market is not a particularly good strategy for preventing imitation, and that the introduction of new ways of organizing, new production processes, and the use of new materials are often easier to defend against imitation than the creation of new products. As is explained in chapter 7, unless the entrepreneur can obtain a patent to protect the new product or service, secrecy is the greatest barrier to the imitation of an entrepreneur's product or service. Because new products and services are things that are provided to customers, it is very hard to keep their workings secret. Competitors can always buy a new product and reverse engineer it. However, new ways of organizing, new raw materials, and new production processes can be kept hidden from customers and competitors. By producing an old product with new ways of organizing, new raw materials, and new production processes, the entrepreneur can ensure that the valuable part of the new business is kept away from competitors' eyes, thereby enhancing performance of the new venture. In fact, academic research on this question has shown that it

Stop! Don't Do It!

1. Don't start a business until you know what form of opportunity is best to exploit it.

2. Don't default to introducing a new product or serving a new market; oftentimes you will be better off developing a new way of organizing, introducing a new raw material, or using a new production process to provide an old product or service.

takes more time, is harder, and costs more for competitors to imitate new production processes than new products and services.[6]

Other differences between new products and other forms of opportunity are also important. It may be easier for entrepreneurs to demonstrate value to potential customers by targeting a new market with an existing product or service than it is to create a new product or service for an old market. In addition, it may be easier to organize and deliver products or services to customers to exploit new markets or create new products or exploit new materials than those that are based on new production processes or new ways to organize.

Types of Opportunities and the Relationship to Types of Innovation

Another important step in the process of identifying valuable opportunities requires you to understand the relationship between these five types of opportunity and the particular forms of innovation through which change operates. Certain types of innovation make possible particular types of opportunities. Successful entrepreneurs know how to match innovation to types of opportunity because new businesses perform better when types of opportunities are matched to innovations than when they are not.

Certain types of innovation can be linked to specific types of opportunities. Altering product dimensions and improving physical properties of products are more likely to lead to new products or services as a type of opportunity. Shifting to continuous production processes, improving process yields, mechanization, automation and standardization tend to generate opportunities in new production processes. Changes in the scale or form of production tend to generate opportunities that take the form of new ways to organize. Designing for new market segments and customization for individual customers tend to result in opportunities to create new markets. Improving inputs are more likely to result in opportunities for raw materials than other forms of opportunities.[7]

These patterns are important to you, as a technology entrepreneur, for a couple of reasons. You need to think about the fact that entrepreneurial opportunities take different forms, and you need to be aware of the way in which different innovations affect those forms of opportunity. Otherwise, you will try to develop opportunities that disproportionately take the form of new products and services when that form of opportunity is inappropriate for the type of innovation that is driving the opportunity.

The types of innovation that leads to these five types of opportunity are not evenly distributed across all industries. As a result, you need to think about exploiting certain types of innovations and not others depending on the industry that you are targeting. For instance, Alvin Klevorick, a professor at Yale University and his colleagues explain that enhancing production scale tends to occur most often in industries like aluminum smelting. Mechanization and automation are very common in making radio and television sets and automobiles. Improving process yield tends to occur in industries like semiconductors. Improving input materials is common in making ball bearings and transformers. Shifting to continuous processes is very common in the production of foods. Changes in product dimensions occur very often in computers', whereas improving the product's

> ## Stop! Don't Do It!
>
> 1. Don't ignore the relationship between types of innovation and forms of opportunity exploitation.
> 2. Don't exploit an innovation that is inappropriate in the industry you are entering.

physical properties is common in rubber and plastics. Improving product performance is common in synthetic fibers; whereas moving toward standardization is found in refrigeration and heating equipment. Designing for market segments is disproportionately represented in paints and cosmetics; whereas tailoring for individual customers tends to occur in mining machinery and turbines.[8]

Locus of Innovation

Another step in identifying a valuable opportunity lies in figuring out what organizations undertake the innovation that creates the opportunity that you intend to pursue. Innovation occurs in different entities that can be thought of as a chain that runs from universities and public research laboratories, which conduct most basic research, to end customers. In the middle are the set of suppliers that provide inputs and other raw materials to companies that produce a good or service, followed by producers.

Understanding this innovation chain is important for three reasons. Different types of innovations tend to occur at different stages in the chain. Therefore, the entities that undertake the innovation that results in entrepreneurial opportunities are different for different industries. For example, universities often undertake the innovation that results in the creation of new scientific instruments. However, semiconductor firms themselves are the entities that typically undertake the innovation that results in improvements in that industry.[9]

The innovations that tend to lead to new firms are those that occur at the basic research end of the spectrum, as well as among suppliers and customers. In general, innovation by firms and their competitors are not as useful for creating new firms. Therefore, successful entrepreneurs tend to focus on innovations in basic research or among suppliers and customers, leaving innovation by firms and their competitors aside, unless that innovation exploits a weakness of established firms (more about that in chapter 6).

One reason for this focus on certain stages in the innovation chain is that entrepreneurs obtain the information that they use to create their new ventures in one of two ways. Either they get that information from knowledge spillovers from established firms or from public entities. Spillovers from established firms occur because those firms have trouble capturing all of their innovation and keeping it inside of the firm. For instance, the Ethernet, the graphical user interface, and the computer mouse were all developed at Xerox Corporation. However, all of them were exploited by new companies rather than by Xerox because the knowledge about how to exploit these innovations leaked out of Xerox. Why? Often employees, customers, or suppliers know about a company's innovation and can make use of it to develop new products or services. As a result, employees, customers, or suppliers can become entrepreneurs.

Sometimes, as in the Xerox case, the employees presented the opportunities to senior management, and senior management chose not to pursue them. In other cases, the employees (or customers and suppliers) do not even bother to tell senior management of a company about the opportunities and simply go after them. Regardless of whether employees, suppliers, and customers advised senior management of a company about opportunities that they have identified, it is often very difficult for firms to prevent knowledge about innovation from spilling over to would-be entrepreneurs.

Stop! Don't Do It!

1. Don't forget opportunities based on innovations by universities and government agencies.

2. Don't start a firm to exploit an innovation that is best developed by an established firm unless you have identified a weakness in the established firm's approach to innovation.

Information used by entrepreneurs also comes from public sector technology developed in universities or government labs. Take the Internet start-ups as an example. The original technological development that led to these companies was the ARPANET, a defense department project. Many entrepreneurs made use of this knowledge to create new technology-based companies. Of course, Netscape, which made a Web browser based on this technology, is probably the most famous of these companies.

A reason for you to understand this innovation chain is that different industries tend to generate innovations at different stages of the chain, indicating that some industries are better for establishing new firms than others.[10] Because new firms are better at exploiting opportunities based on innovations by public entities, suppliers, and customers, new firms do better in industries such as medical devices and computers than in other industries.

Recognizing a Valuable Opportunity

A next step in the process of identifying a valuable opportunity lies in recognizing that an opportunity exists. Often people realize with hindsight that they missed a very valuable opportunity for a new technology business that someone else has exploited. So, why do some people and not others discover valuable opportunities? To answer this question, it is important to remember that entrepreneurial opportunities

exist because of changes in information about such things as technological change, industry structure, social and demographic trends, and
political and regulatory changes. It stands to reason that access to
information or the ability to process it are the key to what make opportunity recognition possible.[11] For instance, some people are the first to
learn about a technological discovery, perhaps because they are working in a research laboratory where an invention is made. The access to
this information before others can learn about it allows people to make
better decisions than others about creating and selling new products.

Access to Information

Some people have better access than others to information about the
changes that open up entrepreneurial opportunities. Several factors
appear to be very important, and successful entrepreneurs make use
of these factors to identify valuable opportunities. Some people have
better positions in social networks. Being positioned well in a social
network allows a person to gain access to information that others cannot access because information is often transmitted through people's
social ties. Friends and acquaintances often tell you things that you
cannot learn in other ways, like the fact that a storefront is going to
become vacant in a few months or that a new technology was
invented. If you have the right ties and others do not, you can gain
access to information that other people cannot tap. Moreover, strong
social ties enhance the transfer of information from one person to
another by making people more willing to believe information trans-
ferred under conditions of uncertainty. People find it difficult to
know whether the information that they hear is accurate. For
instance, is a new technological discovery—say cold fusion—real or a
hoax? To figure out if information is accurate, most people rely on
their friends and trusted others to figure out what information to
believe. Therefore, people with strong social ties to the sources of

information about key changes that serve as sources of opportunities can often get access to that information while other people cannot.

Some people have jobs or life activities that put them closer than others to the source of information about the changes that open up opportunities.[12] For the creation of high-technology businesses, jobs in research and development and marketing appear to be particularly useful in providing access to information about the changes that open up opportunities.[13] Research and development jobs provide information about newly developed technologies that create the opportunity for new businesses. Marketing jobs provide information about customer preferences or unmet customer needs. As a result, these jobs are very helpful in putting people in the flow of information that helps to learn about opportunities to found new firms.

This is not to say that other jobs do not generate access to information about entrepreneurial opportunity. While marketing and R&D provide access to more of that information on average, the appropriate information actually depends on the nature of the opportunity. For instance, an accountant might know about the opportunity to create a business to provide accounting software because they work in the finance unit of a company, not marketing or research and development. However, on average, R&D and marketing jobs provide greater access to information about entrepreneurial opportunity than other jobs.

Also, some people have access to information that others do not have about the changes that generate opportunities because they search for that information. While random searching will not help you to gain access to information that triggers opportunities, targeted efforts to find a solution to technical or market problems can provide valuable information about the sources of opportunity. For example, biotechnology researchers in many universities are currently searching for cures to cancer. They know that finding a cure for cancer will allow them to start a company to exploit that cure. In essence, they are searching for the source of entrepreneurial opportunity.

Better Information Processing

Access to information is only part of the explanation for why some people and not others identify opportunities for new businesses. Another important part is that they are better able to formulate new business ideas from pieces of information about the changes that make new businesses possible. This part is not trivial. Just because you know that a new technology exists doesn't mean that you will be able to think of a business to exploit it. Take, for example, the Swiss watchmakers who invented the digital watch technology. Because these watchmakers couldn't figure out how to use this technology to make watches, they effectively gave away the technology to Japanese companies, who figured out how to commercialize it.

Several aspects of people's mental capabilities influence information processing and help them to recognize entrepreneurial opportunities. Some people have mental schemas about markets and the ways to serve them that allow them to understand and use information in ways that other people cannot.[14] The information that leads to the recognition of an entrepreneurial opportunity does not come in the form of a prepackaged product or service ready for introduction. Rather, it comes as a hint or trigger that something could be done to create a new business given the new technology, new regulation, new industry structure, or new demographic trend. Therefore, identifying valuable business opportunities is a mental process that involves extrapolating from bits and pieces of information.[15]

Schemas are mental frameworks that come from experience that allow people to organize and use information. Research has shown that prior knowledge about markets, either as a customer or supplier, and prior knowledge about how to serve those markets are important sources of useful schemas that will help you to recognize opportunities. For example, if you have knowledge of a customer problem in the automobile industry you will be more likely to figure out the opportunity to create a new automotive business inherent in information about a new material being invented than other people, who are uninformed about the automobile market.

Another mental attribute that allows people to identify opportunities for new businesses is a mind-set that allows a person to see information as generating opportunities, as opposed to creating risks. That person sees entrepreneurial opportunities in new technology. The introduction of new products and services is uncertain because one does not know for sure whether a new product can be created, whether anyone will buy it, or whether competitors will capture the returns by imitating the entrepreneur's new product or service. Therefore, a big part of the identification of an opportunity for a new business involves being willing to see the potential for an opportunity when uncertainties abound.

Academic research has provided support for this observation. For example, one study gave simulation exercises to expert entrepreneurs and bankers. The bankers reported seeing risks where the entrepreneurs reported seeing opportunities.[16] These types of patterns suggest that entrepreneurs have a different way of viewing information that helps them to identify valuable opportunities.

Finally, successful entrepreneurs appear to have a better ability than other people to think up ways to use information that they have gathered about opportunities, perhaps because of their creativity.[17] Creativity facilitates the human ability to combine information, as

Stop! Don't Do It!

1. Don't pick jobs, social networks, or life activities that put you out of the flow of information about new business opportunities.

2. Don't develop a mind-set or way of thinking that keeps you from recognizing entrepreneurial opportunities when you come across them.

well as to see patterns in information that is presented to them. As a result, successful entrepreneurs identify patterns in disparate pieces of information about new technology, market needs, and industry structure and create ideas for new products and services in response to that information that less creative individuals often miss.

In short, some people and not others identify new high-technology business opportunities because they have access to the information about an opportunity opening up and because they have cognitive characteristics that allow them to see those opportunities from bits of information.[18]

Summary

This chapter explained that the second rule for success at technology entrepreneurship is identifying a valuable opportunity. The initial step in this process is to locate the source of the opportunity. A few key primary sources of entrepreneurial opportunities exist, that is, technological change, political/regulatory change, social/demographic change, and change in industrial structure.

Technological change is a source of opportunity because it makes things possible that were not possible before and makes it possible to

Questions to Ask Yourself

1. What is the source of opportunity for my new business?
2. What factors generated this opportunity?
3. What new products, production processes, markets, raw materials, and ways of organizing do these changes make possible?
4. What types of innovation are occurring to make these things happen?
5. What would enable me to spot this opportunity before others do?

do things in more efficient ways. A number of dimensions of techno-logical change influence its value as a source of opportunity: the magnitude of the change, its generality, its commercial viability, and its effect on industrial structure.

Political and regulatory change is a source of opportunity because it makes productivity enhancing activity possible and because it makes it possible to shift value from one economic factor to another. Deregulation creates opportunities by allowing entrants to offer new alternatives. Regulation creates opportunity by increasing demand or offering subsidies that affect the cost-benefit trade-off for products and services.

Social and demographic change is a source of opportunity because it alters preferences, thereby changing demand. Three important types of social and demographic changes that open up entrepreneurial opportunity are demographic shifts, social trends, and exogenous shifts in perceptions.

Changes in industrial structure are a source of entrepreneurial opportunity because they make it possible for new suppliers to enter and because they make it possible to change competitive dynamics.

The second step in the process of identifying valuable opportunities is to figure out the form that the efforts to exploit the opportunity will take. Opportunities do not have to take the form of new products and services. They also take the form of new markets, new raw materials, new production processes, and new ways of organizing. While entrepreneurs typically think in terms of creating new products and services, creating new raw materials, production processes, and ways of organizing may be better for them. One of the key factors affecting entrepreneurial performance is the ability to minimize imitation. Because new raw materials, production processes, and ways of organizing are easier to keep secret than new products, they are better than other forms of opportunity exploitation for minimizing imitation.

A key step in the process of identifying valuable opportunities is to match the forms that opportunities take to specific types of innovation. This is important for a couple of reasons. Fitting the right form of opportunity exploitation to the type of innovation that has occurred enhances the performance of new ventures. The types of innovation are not evenly distributed across industries, indicating that the form of opportunity exploitation that is appropriate for entrepreneurs to pursue depends on the industry in which they operate.

Another step in the process of identifying valuable opportunities is to identify where in the innovation chain the change occurs. This is important because the type of innovation that leads to the opportunity varies by stage of the chain. Moreover, the tendency of people to create new firms in response to these innovations varies across the stage of the innovation chain. Furthermore, the innovation chain indicates that some industries are better than others for creating new firms.

The final step in the process of identifying valuable opportunities is to understand how individuals identify opportunities for new businesses. Factors central to this process are access to information and information-processing capability. Some people are more likely than others to gain access to the information that signals the presence of an entrepreneurial opportunity because of their position in social networks, because of their jobs and life experiences and because of the search processes they adopt. Some people are more likely than others to process information in a way that allows them to identify entrepreneurial opportunities because of their mental schemas, their perception of risk, and their creativity.

Now that you understand rule number two of technology entrepreneurship, identify valuable opportunities, we now turn to rule number three, manage technological evolution, which is the subject of the next chapter.

3

MANAGING
TECHNOLOGICAL
EVOLUTION

While the previous chapter indicated that technological change is a source of entrepreneurial opportunity, the discussion was incomplete. Responding to the right type of technological change is as important, if not more important for successful technology entrepreneurship, than is responding to technological change in general. Successful technological entrepreneurship requires a focus on technological transitions.

This focus on technological transitions is important because, most of the time, entrepreneurs target the wrong type of technological change to establish their new businesses. They start their businesses to exploit incremental change. By focusing on incremental change, entrepreneurs often find that they cannot compete with established firms and fail. What successful technology entrepreneurs have come to realize is that, to be successful, new ventures need to target technological transitions, points when an industry is shifting from one basic technology to another, such as when the printing industry shifted from hot lead linotype machines to cold off-set printing generated by computers.

Your new venture will be greatly advantaged by focusing on technological transitions because they undermine the advantages of established firms. The reluctance of established firms to embrace these transitions will allow you to enter an industry and use the new technology to develop a business that is based on what may ultimately becomes a better technology than that belonging to the established firm. However, these transitions are difficult to manage because they involve improving the new technology from its initial state and timing entry appropriately. Therefore, successful technology entrepreneurs have developed specific strategies for managing technological evolution.

This chapter focuses on explaining several key characteristics of managing the process of technological evolution. The chapter:

- Explains why technologies follow evolutionary patterns that open up discrete points of transition that are valuable for entrepreneurs to exploit

- Describes the S-shaped pattern of technological development and the implications of this pattern for technology entrepreneurs

- Discusses the role of dominant designs and explains how these designs influence competition by entrepreneurial ventures

- Describes technical standards and how entrepreneurs can use strategic action to focus them around their products and services

- Explores increasing returns businesses, explaining both why increasing returns businesses exist, and how entrepreneurs should approach those industries to be successful

Evolutionary Patterns of Development

New technology tends to develop in an evolutionary manner. For example, technological advance in the computer industry has followed a pattern in which microprocessors have become smaller and more powerful because engineers have developed better and better ways of packing more and more onto each microchip.

While scientific, economic, and institutional factors shape the direction in which technology evolves, the evolution depends primarily on the incremental process by which research occurs. Scientists and engineers work within particular frameworks that limit their approaches to problem solving. In particular, these frameworks influence how innovation occurs by affecting the identification of the problems that need to be solved from those that do not. These frameworks have the advantage of keeping researchers focused on the key questions that they need to answer. However, they also limit possibilities. By leading to the creation of a particular outlook on problems, these frameworks create a strong tendency for researchers to ignore certain types of approaches.[1] For example, current technological frameworks view making microchips faster as an electrical problem, not a biological one. As a result, researchers do not work on biological solutions to semiconductor speed.

At discrete points in time, opportunities appear to fundamentally change the technological frameworks that scientists and engineers in

Stop! Don't Do It!

1. Don't focus all of your efforts on an existing technological paradigm. If you do, you will not be able to exploit the new paradigm when it comes along.

2. Don't ignore the changes in technological frameworks that scientists and engineers are using; they often signal new opportunities.

an industry tend to use. For example, the photographic film industry faced a fundamental shift to digital technology from traditional film in the 1990s. Similarly, in the late 1980s, offset printers faced a fundamental shift to desktop publishing from cold type printing. These discrete shifts are important to entrepreneurs because new firms founded to exploit these shifts tend to be the most successful new firms started.

Projecting Foster's S-Curves

The incremental advances that occur within a technological framework and the radical shifts between technology frameworks can be presented graphically using a concept called the S-curve. Developed by Richard Foster, a McKinsey consultant, the S-curve shows the performance of a technology as a function of the amount of effort expended to develop it. That is, an S-curve allows you to show graphically the development of a particular technology.[2]

New technology products and services begin with a very low level of performance on the dimensions that are important to potential customers.[3] The performance of new technology products and services increase as the developers of those technologies invest time and effort in their development, improving them on the dimensions that customers care about. However, initially, the developers of a new technology achieve very little return on the investment of time and money in a new technology. When people first work on advancing a technology, they often spend time on developmental dead ends. Moreover, even when they do not head down dead ends, their progress is slow. As soon as researchers solve one problem, they are confronted with others, leading each problem-solving exercise to yield little in the way of tangible performance improvements. Ultimately, the developers of a new technology achieve breakthroughs that allow for dramatic improvement in performance. This improvement continues until the technology reaches diminishing returns, which then slows the rate of technology improvement. The result is an S-shaped curve of technology development (see Figure 3.1).[4]

The fact that technology development takes on an S-shaped pattern is important to you, as a technology entrepreneur, in several ways. The initial performance improvement of the new technology is so low that the performance of your new products and services is likely to be inferior to that of existing alternatives when it is first introduced. As a result, at first you cannot compete successfully with existing firms on the basis of the new technology. To compete successfully, you have to obtain capital and invest in the further development of the new technology to get it to the point at which your new products and services are competitive with existing alternatives. Take, for example, Internet telephone service. Voice-over Internet Protocol was launched in the 1990s, but companies that exploited it could not compete successfully with traditional telephone companies because the technology required further development before it offered performance that was comparable to traditional telephone service.

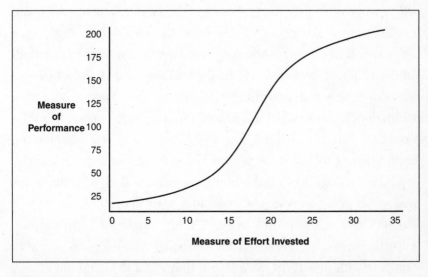

FIGURE 3.1 The S-Shaped Curve of Technology Development

Because of the efforts of a large number of start-ups that invested in the development of this technology, it is now a competitive alternative to conventional telephone technology.

The S-curve signals when an opportunity is likely to open up and allow new firms to enter and compete with established firms. Established firms generally focus on making incremental improvements to an existing technology, a process that leads them to move up the S-curve on which they are already operating.[5] Ultimately, all technologies reach diminishing returns, making it difficult for managers to achieve very marked performance improvement in their technologies. At these points when technologies are facing these diminishing returns, new firms can often successfully enter industries with new technologies.

The S-curve helps you, as a technology entrepreneur, to understand why you, and not established firms, will introduce products and services based on new technologies. Because products and services based on new technology begin with inferior performance to products and services based on existing technology, established firms have little economic incentive to switch from the existing technology to the new technology. The managers of existing companies simply compare the new technology to the technology that they are already using and decide against the change. Moreover, the established firms have investments in existing technology that they do not want to cannibalize by changing technologies, further adding to their reluctance to introduce new technologies. Furthermore, the crudeness of new technology when it is first introduced often leads the managers of the established firms to believe that a new technology will have limited application. The failure to project the potential of new technology leads the managers of established companies to stick with the status quo when doing so does not make long-term sense. Finally, even if the new technology proves to be of value, established firms always have the option of improving their existing technology as a way to compete with new firms. As a result, they resist the adoption of new technology. In short, you and other technology entrepreneurs like you are much more likely than established firms to be the ones to introduce new technology products and services.

The S-curve highlights the importance of timing the entry of your new business into an industry. Because the improvement in the performance of the new technology takes an S-shaped pattern, not a linear form, it is important for you to figure out when the performance of a new technology will accelerate. This tells you the right moment to enter. Entering too early will saddle your new venture with costs before it has a technology that is better than that offered by established firm competitors, allowing established firm competitors to drive you out of business. Entering too late will allow other new firms to enter before you do and gain the advantages of being a first mover.

E-books provide a good example of S-curves and the problem of timing market entry. For several years, people have been saying that electronic books will replace paper books. However, to date, the performance of E-books—ease of use, availability of titles, and so on—has not exceeded that of paper books, and the rate of performance improvement in them has been rather slow. As a result, most E-book publishing companies that have been founded have run into financial trouble. Why? The entrepreneurs who founded these companies have mistimed the S-curve. They have entered the market too early

Stop! Don't Do It!

1. Don't expect your new products to be as good initially as those of established companies if you start a company to exploit a new technology.

2. Don't enter an industry too soon after its core technology changes.

3. Don't wait too long to enter an industry after its core technology changes.

in its growth. By entering before the acceleration point of the S-curve, the entrepreneurs have been saddled with technology that is not superior to that of competitors, leading them to run out of cash before they can come up with a product that is competitive with paper book technology.

The Role of Dominant Designs

Another important issue for you to consider in managing the process of technology evolution is that many new technologies converge on dominant designs, or common way that all companies producing a product will design their version, and that convergence dramatically changes the nature of competition in an industry.[6] The internal combustion engine in automobiles is a good example of a dominant design. All automakers produce vehicles with internal combustion engines. The alternatives of steam-powered engines that once existed are long gone.

Dominant designs matter to you, as a technology entrepreneur, because the way in which firms compete depends largely on whether a dominant design exists. Technology evolves through periods of incremental change, interrupted by radical developments. During periods of incremental change, one design is dominant in an industry. A radical development ushers in an era of change in which many designs compete. Ultimately, a convergence on a dominant product design occurs.[7]

In general, the conditions that exist before a dominant design emerges are more favorable to new firms than conditions that exist after a dominant design emerges. Before a dominant design emerges, barriers to entry are low, facilitating firm formation at a lower cost, and therefore a lower risk. Markets are also fragmented, with many small competitors. Because of this fragmentation, it is hard for firms to grow large, and few competitors have scale economies, or try to compete on the basis of the efficiency of producing standardized products. As a result, new firms, which will lack scale economies and high levels of manufacturing efficiency, at least initially, are less disadvantaged than they would be if production were not fragmented. Moreover, because firms in the predominant design phase are not hindered by having to adopt a product design that is the same as that belonging to more experienced firms, competition occurs on the basis of varied product design. This, too, favors new firms, which have the nonhierarchical organization structures that facilitate product design and development.

However, once a dominant design emerges, firms can no longer compete on the basis of variation in design and, instead, have to compete on cost. The existence of a dominant design allows firms to exploit economies of scale and become efficient in manufacturing, making it hard for new firms to match the advantages of existing firms.[8] As a result, once a dominant design is in place, industries consolidate around a small number of larger firms. The number of competing firms in an industry drops dramatically, with estimates of the drop in the number of firms in an industry from the peak level to a stable level averaging 52 percent and ranging as high as 87 percent.[9]

The story of electric vehicles is one that illustrates the concept of convergence on a dominant design. David Kirsch, a business historian, explains that, in 1900, gasoline powered vehicles were actually less common than steam and electric powered vehicles.[10] Although electric and steam vehicles had many technical advantages over gasoline powered vehicles, they were not as effective for touring. As a result, people began to favor gasoline-powered cars. Over time, as gasoline-powered cars became the most popular, manufacturers designed fewer and fewer steam and electric powered vehicles and those who did tended to fail. As a result, the automobile industry converged on a dominant design in gasoline powered engines in the early part of the twentieth century, and this design has remained dominant ever since.

Because dominant designs are important to entrepreneurial performance, successful entrepreneurs understand why dominant designs emerge. In some cases, chance occurrences can lead to their formation. That is, we end up with a dominant design because that design was in the right place at the right time. This cause, of course, is the hardest cause for you to manage because you cannot influence chance. However, it is important for you to understand, nonetheless.

Social, political, and organizational factors can lead to the creation of a dominant design. For example, as was mentioned earlier, one reason we ended up with the internal combustion engine being the dominant design in automobiles was that, at the beginning of the twentieth century, people used their automobiles largely for touring. This social factor made gasoline-powered engines better than electric-powered ones because the latter needed recharging, which was hard to do in the countryside.[11] Because social, political, and organizational factors influence the convergence of a technology on a dominant design, you can benefit from understanding the way in which these factors influence the development of a dominant design in an industry.

The nature of the technology can lend itself to the formation of a dominant design. For example, the chemical makeup of synthetic fibers means that only a few of them—nylon and polyester, for instance—can produce long fibers. As a result, nylon and polyesters are the dominant designs of synthetic fibers.[12] You can therefore evaluate the nature of the technologies on which you are working to determine whether it is likely to converge on a dominant design.

Dominant designs also have two important characteristics in common that you need to remember. Dominant designs are not technologies at the frontier of knowledge. State-of-the-art designs achieve superior performance through experimental advances that are too unreliable for the majority of customers. As a result, dominant designs are rarely cutting edge technologies, fitting the needs of the majority of adopters, rather than the lead users. The radical develop-

Stop! Don't Do It!

1. Don't expect technology alone to determine the dominant design; remember social and political factors matter.

2. Don't expect a new technology that led to a radical shift in an industry to become the dominant design.

ments that led to the formation of an era of change also rarely become dominant designs. Why? Because the technologies that become dominant designs are generally shaped by technological variation during the era of change, and it is very hard for a radical technological change to pass through the era of change without undergoing modification.

Understanding Technical Standards

Many new technology products and services must adhere to a technical standard, or an agreed-upon basis on which a product or service operates. A good example of a technical standard is the electrical outlet. All electronic devices have plugs that fit exactly the same technical standard. This ensures that all electronic devices fit into all outlets.

Technical standards are important to you, as a technology entrepreneur, for several reasons. Companies that produce products that become a technical standard are often incredibly successful. Why? Because all other companies have to design complementary products to fit the technical standard. As a result, the company that controls the standard can earn high margins on its product. Take the Windows operating system as an example. Because 80 percent of the world's computers use the Windows operating system, Microsoft can earn high margins on that system.

Technical standards often mean that you can sell products and services that are technically inferior to alternative products or services even if a superior technology comes along. The standard typewriter keyboard is a good example of what I mean. The standard QWERTY keyboard was designed initially to *slow* typing, which was important with typewriters of the 1880s that were prone to jamming. However, by the 1930s, several superior keyboard designs had been patented. In fact, one of these keyboards, patented by Dvorak and Dealey in 1932, was so good that the costs of retraining typists to use it could be amortized in ten days. However, the new keyboards have never been adopted—even today when all one has to do is flick a switch on one's computer to change keyboards—because the QWERTY keyboard is a technical standard. People stay with it, despite its technical inferiority, because that keyboard is complementary to hardware manufacturers and touch-typing trainers who can assume that everyone is following the same technical standard if the world remains set on the QWERTY keyboard.[13]

Failure to adhere to a technical standard can create great problems for entrepreneurs because customers naturally move toward suppliers that adhere to the technical standard. Take, for example, the experience of Scott McNealy at Sun Microsystems. For years, Sun has developed custom microchips that are more powerful and more expensive than competitors' chips. Initially, Sun found a performance niche in the powerful computers that run network servers. However, eventually these computers, like others, have converged on the Intel chip standard. As a result, Sun has suffered recently from very large declines in sales, and was forced to adopt the technical standard to survive.[14]

Given that technical standards are important to entrepreneurs; you need to know how they get established. Research has shown that four ways predominate. Initially, a group of firms agree to adopt a standard. Oftentimes this means that the leading firms in an industry get together and decide on the standard for the technology that they are all using. For example, in the case of electrical engineering, the IEEE has many standards committees formed with this function in mind. Other times, the government imposes a standard, as would be the case if a government mandated that all firms use a particular telecommunications protocol to ensure that all consumers can communicate with each other. Sometimes, the technology itself motivates the creation of standard. This tends to occur when the technology has network externalities or faces increasing returns. Finally, the strategic actions of an entrepreneur drive an industry to a standard.

The use of strategic actions to make a firm's product or service a technical standard begs the question: What actions should you take when you found your company to make your new product or service the technical standard? After all, as I said earlier, firms that control the technical standard often earn very high margins. The best actions for you to take all revolve around getting more customers faster than competitors. One way to do this is to offer a low price to generate a high volume of customers. A high volume of customers attracts suppliers of complementary products and services, which makes the entrepreneur's product or service more attractive. Take Microsoft as an example. Because Microsoft attracted more customers to its operating system than its competitors did to theirs, more suppliers were willing to provide Microsoft with software applications, which made it a more attractive operating system to consumers than the Apple operating system. As a result, Windows became the technical standard for software makers.[15]

You can work with the producers of complementary technologies in other ways to make your products or services more attractive to customers, as was the case with the makers of VHS videocassette recorders. Videocassette recorders are complementary technologies to movies and other material recorded on the tapes. The VHS videocassette format became the technical standard, rather than the alternative of Betamax, because the companies producing the VHS format worked much harder than Sony to get producers of movies to record

Stop! Don't Do It!

1. Don't fail to adhere to technical standards when creating your product or service.

2. Don't ignore the role of strategic action in creating a technical standard.

their movies in VHS format. As a result, more movies were available for VHS than for Betamax, encouraging the adoption of VHS as the technical standard.[16]

Another way that you can increase the likelihood that your product becomes the technical standard is to build sales quickly. Because it is easier to converge on a high-volume product as a technical standard than on a low-volume product, sales volume is important to making a product a technical standard. To do this, you will need to begin by introducing a simple version of their product with limited features to allow high-volume mass production to occur more quickly.[17]

Evolution in Increasing Returns Businesses

Academics used to believe that all business was based on a concept of decreasing returns. Decreasing returns means that the more of something that you produce, the lower the returns that you will achieve on that production. A good example of decreasing returns is mining. At first, when you mine a vein of coal or gold, you get a high return because you tap the least costly veins. Over time, however, as you produce more and more coal or gold, you use up the easy-to-access material and are forced to incur higher and higher costs to get the remaining deposits. As a result, costs increase, causing decreasing returns. While many industries—mining, heavy chemicals, agriculture, construction—display decreasing returns, researchers have recently discovered that many high-technology businesses display increasing returns.[18]

Increasing returns businesses are those in which the benefits of something increase as the volume of production increases. Software is a good example of a business based on increasing returns. The more software you produce, the higher your returns on sales will be because virtually all of the costs of producing software lie in the production of the first unit. Once initial costs of writing code have been paid for, it costs only pennies to stamp an additional compact disk with software. Researchers have found that many knowledge-based technology businesses—pharmaceuticals, computers, and telecommunication to name a few—display increasing returns.

Okay, so why do some industries, and not others, display increasing returns? The first reason was suggested earlier. When up-front costs are high, and marginal costs are small, unit costs drop dramatically as volume increases. As a result, increasing returns are present. Take, for example, drug production. It costs hundreds of millions of dollars to research and test a new drug. However, once that drug has achieved FDA approval, most of the costs have been incurred. The cost of producing each capsule of a drug is very small. The more of a drug that is produced, the higher is the profit margin on drug sales.

Another reason is network externalities. Network externalities describe a situation in which the value of a product or service increase with the number of people using it. Take e-mail as an example. When only a handful of people had e-mail, it was a much less valuable communication tool than it is now that large numbers of people have it. Why? When only a handful of people had e-mail, people could not assume that e-mail could be used as a way to communicate, reducing the value of the tool.

Increasing returns exist in some industries because complementary technologies are important in those industries. When complementary technologies exist—things like computer hardware and computer software that together help people achieve their goals—the value of both technologies increase with volume. A good example of this is the relationship between broadband Internet connections and voice-over Internet protocol. As broadband access becomes more pervasive, the ability to use the Internet for telephone conversations increases, facilitating the development of that product.

Increasing returns exist in some industries and not others because producer learning is high. When firms can learn a great deal by operating their businesses, efficiency increases significantly with production levels. So, the more a firm produces, the lower its costs become, and the higher its profit margins.

Increasing returns also exist in some industries and not others because switching costs are high. If it is expensive to switch from one product or service to another, customers become "locked in" to the product or service they are using. If switching costs are high, the customer is always better off remaining with the product or service that they have rather than incurring the cost of switching. If people do not switch, this benefits the firm producing the product or service.

Increasing returns are important for you to understand if you want to become a successful technology entrepreneur because starting companies in industries based on increasing returns is a very different from starting companies in industries based on decreasing returns. In industries based on increasing returns, "first mover" advantages—the benefits of providing the first product or service in a market—are very important. Early success often generates later success because the firms that have more customers initially face lower costs than those who have fewer customers initially. eBay, the Internet auction house, provides a good example. Because eBay was one of the first Internet auction houses, it garnered the first customers. By virtue of having those customers, other people were attracted to sell their things on eBay (the most customers were already going there), which allowed eBay to earn higher margins than other Internet auction houses and kept them ahead of the competition.

Because first mover advantages are so important in industries based on increasing returns, waiting until one has the best technology is not a very effective strategy in these industries. If you delay the launch of your new product or service until you have perfected your technology and made it is superior to that offered by competitors, you will have a lot of problems in an increasing returns business. In these businesses, the best technologies may not win out. If customers do not find it worthwhile to switch from another product to yours, they will often remain with the inferior technology after your superior technology has been introduced. As a result, a better strategy for you to follow in these industries is to get to market quickly with whatever products you have, and then try to improve your products in the process of operating your business.

This, of course, is standard operating procedure in the software industry. Knowing that software is an industry based on increasing returns, most successful entrepreneurs in that industry start out by launching beta versions that need significant technical improvement. They then improve their software over time while operating their businesses. These entrepreneurs have the comfort of knowing that it is very costly for customers to switch from their products to those of competitors, allowing the strategy to work.

The strategy of entrepreneurs in increasing returns businesses differs from that of entrepreneurs in decreasing returns businesses because of the importance of generating customer lock in. Because returns increase with the volume sold, locking in customers is important to enhancing financial returns.

One way to get customers locked into a product or service is to use a "razor blade model." Named after the early safety razor companies who used to sell their razors at close to cost and then make all of their profit on the sales of blades that were uniquely designed for their razors, this approach leads customers to become locked into the replacement components that belong to the company that supplied them with the initial system. Once customers have purchased the initial system, they are usually better off buying the components to that system rather than changing systems, even if the components cost more than those offered by competitors.

If your new product has one component that is purchased up front and another component that is purchased repeatedly over time, the best strategy for you to follow is to offer the up-front component at a low cost to lure the customer in. If the customer gets locked in, then the component purchased repeatedly over time can be sold at a high margin. A good example of this strategy is that used by video game manufacturers. Most of the devices to play video games are sold at very close to cost, but the software that plays the games is sold at high margins. Once people have purchased a particular video game device, they have high costs to switching to another one, allowing the video game manufacturers to sell the game cartridges at a high price.

Offering the up-front component at a low cost is central to this strategy for two reasons. Most new technology products are uncertain. Customers do not know if they will have value until they use them. Therefore, a low price is necessary to get them to try the system and see if it has value. Most customers are myopic. They will generally underestimate how many units of a product they will purchase over time, particularly if there is uncertainty initially about the value of the product. As a result, they will almost always select a product with a low-cost initial component and a high-cost recurring purchase component over a high-cost initial component and a low-cost recurring purchase component because they will believe that the first one is less expensive than the second.

Another important aspect of strategy for you to follow in increasing returns businesses is to take actions to ensure that complementary technology is developed. As a result, open systems strategies work very well in increasing returns businesses. By making your technology open for others to see, you can make it possible for the producers of complementary technologies to understand how to provide complementary technologies. This, of course, will increase the likelihood that complementary technologies are available; and the availability of complementary technologies, in turn, will generate increasing returns.

The benefits of producing a product or service in an increasing returns business are also enhanced by strategic partnering. A firm can get its products or services to market more quickly by contracting with other firms to produce those products or services for it than it can by producing those products or services on its own. This approach is very effective in increasing returns businesses because volume production and first mover advantages provide such high benefits in these types of businesses. This, of course, is why so many new companies in industries, such as software, are virtual companies, in which new firms do not establish production, but license to, or form strategic alliances with, other firms to produce their software for them.

Another aspect of strategy for you to follow in increasing returns businesses is to make large bets.[19] There are a few reasons why. To be successful in these types of industries, you need to attract customers first, and make profits second, so these businesses experience high levels of negative cash flow. As a result, these businesses need deep-pocketed investors who will bet significant amounts of money on the businesses.

There is no reason for you to start small in an increasing returns business. If a technology offers increasing returns, there is significant value to having a high volume of production. As a result, starting a small business and bootstrapping it is not a very effective strategy in these industries. Starting on a small scale would lead you to miss out on the first mover advantages and the lock in of many customers that are central to success in increasing returns businesses. Therefore, you need to make large magnitude investments in increasing returns businesses.

Stop! Don't Do It!

1. Don't adopt a decreasing returns business strategy in an increasing returns business.

2. Don't try to exploit an increasing returns business on a small scale.

Increasing returns businesses are winner-take-all businesses. Because the most successful firms in increasing returns businesses have much lower cost structures than competitors, these businesses tend toward natural monopolies in which the products of the most successful firms become de facto technical standards. As a result, the new ventures either control the market and earn high margins, or they tend to fail.

Of course, these businesses are not for the faint of heart. Businesses in which people make larger investments to try to dominate a market are riskier than other businesses because the ventures can fail and the downside loss from failure is higher if more has been

Questions to Ask Yourself

1. Is the industry I am thinking of entering facing a technological transition?

2. What is the pace of technological progress in my industry?

3. Has a dominant design or technical standard emerged?

4. If not, what can I do to make my product the dominant design or technical standard?

5. Is the business I am entering an increasing or decreasing returns business?

6. If it is an increasing returns business, what should I do to capitalize on that?

invested. Therefore, the large bets in increasing returns businesses are important to success, but risky nonetheless. In fact, the Internet grocery delivery start-up, Webvan, provides an example of the magnitude of the risk that entrepreneurs and their investors face when starting a new company in an increasing returns business. The investors in this company lost several hundred million dollars of investors' money when this venture failed.

Summary

Technological development follows an evolutionary pattern in which scientists and engineers work within frameworks that limit problem-solving approaches to a prevailing paradigm. At certain points in time, new technologies appear that radically shift the underlying technological paradigm. These radical shifts provide an excellent opportunity for entrepreneurs to enter industries, as long as they can successfully manage the technological transition.

Managing a technological transition first requires you to understand Foster's technological development S-curve. The S-curve shows that technologies initially experience slow performance improvement because of the process of learning. Then breakthroughs are made and technologies improve dramatically. In the final phase, improvement slows as laws of diminishing returns kick in. At this point a new technology often appears, leading to a transition to a new S-curve.

As a technology entrepreneur, Foster's S-curve has several implications for you. The transition to a new S-curve is almost always undertaken by new firms rather than established firms, which have little incentive to make the transition. The new technology generally begins with worse performance than the old technology, making it very difficult for the new firm to compete initially with established firms. The timing of new firm entry is important. Too early entry means too slow technology improvement for new firms to be competitive with established firms using the old technology, and too late entry means a missed opportunity to other entrepreneurs entering with the new technology.

Managing technological evolution also involves understanding dominant designs and how they influence competition by new and established firms in an industry. New firms tend to perform better before a dominant design has been established than after a dominant design is in place because prior to convergence on dominant designs, barriers to entry are low, product competition is strong, learning curves are limited, efficiency is relatively unimportant, and organizational hierarchies are not effective in the predominant design phase. All of these things favor new firms over established ones.

Managing technological evolution requires you to consider the role of technical standards. Technical standards are created by firm agreement, government action, the characteristics of technology itself, and the strategic actions of entrepreneurs. Because establishing a firm's product as the technical standard generates large financial returns to entrepreneurial activity, successful entrepreneurs often take specific strategic actions to make their product a technical standard: adopting a low price, making their new products and services work effectively with complementary technologies, and launching simple products.

A final aspect of managing technological evolution that is important for you to consider is managing the differences in the pattern of development of increasing and decreasing returns businesses. Businesses have increasing returns when up-front costs are high relative to marginal costs, when network externalities are present, when complementary technologies are important to the effective use of a product or service, when producer learning is strong, and when switching costs are high. Under conditions of increasing returns, an effective entrepreneurial strategy involves achieving a first mover advantage, partnering early with the producers of complementary technologies, and betting aggressively.

Now that you understand rule number three of technology entrepreneurship, manage technological evolution, we now turn to rule number four, identify and satisfy real market needs, which is the subject of the next chapter.

4

IDENTIFYING AND SATISFYING REAL MARKET NEEDS

To create a successful new high-technology company, you need to introduce a product or service that satisfies customer needs in a better way than competitors, and at a price that is greater than the cost of creating that product or service. While, in principle, this objective might seem easy to achieve, in practice it is not. You need to identify *real* customer needs and provide products or services that meet those needs in ways that were previously unmet, or meet those needs in ways that are significantly better than the alternatives offered by competing firms.

You need to evaluate customer preferences for the features of the new products and services that they offer. Because many new technology products and services create new markets or radically transform existing markets, this process of evaluating customer preferences is difficult, and requires you to use market research techniques that go beyond the focus groups and surveys with which you are probably most familiar.

You need to understand how to price and sell new technology products and services. This involves learning about the purchasing decisions of prospective customers and how users are sometimes, but not always, the purchasers of new technology. It also involves learning how to employ personal selling techniques effectively, rather than relying on advertising or brand-name reputation to sell new products and services. Finally, it involves accurate pricing of new technology products and services.

This chapter discusses all these topics. It begins with identifying a real need for new products and services.

Identifying a Real Need

Successful technology entrepreneurs launch companies that offer new products and services that meet a *real* customer need. While this point might seem pretty obvious, it needs to be made. Most technology entrepreneurs do not offer new products and services that meet real customer needs. As a result, their companies generate few sales and go nowhere.

If it is important for you, as a technology entrepreneur, to introduce new products and services that meet real needs, how do you figure if there is a real customer need for the products or services that you have created? By answering basic questions. Do customers have an unsolved problem that no existing product or service solves? If no existing product or service solves a problem that customers are looking to have solved, then a real need exists. For example, a noninvasive home test that detects hypertension would be an example of a medical test that meets a real need. There is currently no way for people to test themselves for hypertension and allow this problem to be treated before it causes serious damage.

Another basic question to ask is if there is a significantly better way of solving a customer's problem than an existing product or service provides? A real need also exists if a new product or service is significantly better at solving a customer's problem than competing products or service on dimensions that customers consider important. Notice the use of the word *significantly* in the previous two sentences. For a real need to exist, the new product or service cannot just be a little bit better than the existing alternative. People tend to require a pretty high hurdle to undertake change, and so will not undertake it for only a slight benefit. For example, an automobile engine design that doubles fuel efficiency would likely meet a real need, but one that increased fuel efficiency by just 1 percent probably would not.

As you might have surmised from this discussion of real needs, successfully introducing a new product or service is much easier if you start with a customer problem. Obviously, it is much easier to find a way to solve a known problem than an unknown one. Most successful technology entrepreneurs realize this and act accordingly. They think of new products or services to introduce by looking to potential customers for clues the customers have an unsolved or poorly solved problem.

Potential customers often provide clues to indicate the presence of an unsolved problem. The best clue is a customer complaint. A complaint indicates that a potential customer is unhappy with the status quo. Take, for example, the case of underwriters at several insurance companies who complain that the software that they use to check the driving records of new clients is hard to use and inaccurate. The fact that several underwriters complain that they face the same problem indicates that there is a need for a better solution.

Another clue to the presence of a customer problem is the expression of an unfulfilled wish. An unfulfilled wish indicates that a customer would do something differently only if there were a way to do it. A good example of an unfilled wish is the number of people who indicate that they would like to vacation in outer space. The fact that people say that they would like to vacation in space when there is no way to do so at the moment provides evidence of an unmet need for the entrepreneur who comes up with a way to provide "space vacations."

Stop! Don't Do It!

1. Don't start a business with a product that does not meet a real customer need.

2. Don't ignore the clues that potential customers give about what new products and services they need.

Meeting a Real Need

Of course, identifying a customer need is only part of the process of satisfying a real customer need. You also have to come with a product or service that meets the need. After all, identifying a clear market need without coming up with a product or service is just an academic exercise that does nothing for you as an entrepreneur.

Therefore, after a real need is identified, you need to develop a product or service that meets the need. Take the space tourism example from earlier. Suppose you are the entrepreneur in this example. How are you planning to get people into space? Are you going to rent seats on NASA's space shuttle? Or are you going to build a launch vehicle? If you are going to build a launch, is it going to be a rocket or an airplanelike vehicle? You would need to answer these questions if you are to come up with a product that meets customer needs in the space tourism business.

Gathering Information about Customer Preferences

To design a product that meets a customer need, you need to gather detailed information about customer preferences. While this sounds like a straightforward activity, in reality, it is not. Unlike evaluating customer preferences for refinements to existing products and services, evaluating customer preferences for new products and services

Stop! Don't Do It!

1. Don't try to meet customer needs that you can't solve with the products and services you can create.
2. Don't forget to ask yourself how you will meet customer needs.

is hard to do with standard market research tools, such as focus groups and customer surveys. For truly new products and services, which are the ones that entrepreneurs are the most effective at introducing, you need to do things like forecast trends and potential adoption patterns to learn about customer preferences.

Dorothy Leonard, a professor at Harvard Business School, offers several reasons why. When a new product is truly new, the customer may not understand his or her own needs for it. While the customer has a real need, he or she is simply unable to comprehend that need or to articulate it to entrepreneurs.[1] A good example of this phenomenon is the need for Internet shopping. When the Internet was first created, people really did not know how it could be used to meet their shopping needs. As a result, in the beginning, entrepreneurs could not survey people and ask them about buying cars or clothes online as a way to gather information about their needs. At that time, people did not yet understand why they might want to shop online, or even what the concept of online shopping meant.

With truly new products or services, it is hard to know who the right customers are. Take the laser, for example. When this technology was first invented, no one knew what market applications there would be for it. In fact, the patent attorneys at IBM, where it was invented, recommended against patenting because no one at IBM saw any particular market application for the laser. Of course, now we know that the laser has a wide variety of market applications, from making compact disks to supermarket scanners.

It is also difficult to communicate information about a very novel product or service concept. Take, for instance, the invention of the photocopying machine. When this technology was first introduced by Halloid Corporation, the precursor to Xerox, the company had trouble assessing whether potential customers would be interested. At the time that this technology was introduced, people simply could not mechanically reproduce existing documents in libraries, universities, offices, and so on. As a result, it was virtually impossible for the founders of the company to discuss the product concept with the customers who ended up using it. Potential customers did not know that they would have a need for this product because the product needed to be introduced before they could really understand that it could solve the problems that they had in reproducing documents.

Because of the difficulty of communicating product concepts and managing the uncertainty present with new products and services, the process of gathering information about customer preferences for these products and services is very different than for existing products and services, both in terms of the general philosophy underlying the effort and the techniques used by successful entrepreneurs. Given the uncertainty and difficulty in communicating information about new products and services, you need to rely on your own intuition and interpretation to figure out customer preferences for truly new products and services. To do this, you really need to understand the context in which the product will be used so that you can make decisions that really fit the needs of customers. Therefore, successful entrepreneurs tend to rely on deep involvement with the customer in place of just gathering information through customer surveys and

Stop! Don't Do It!

1. Don't use market research techniques designed for known products and markets to gather information about new products and markets.

2. Don't forget to rely on your own intuition in evaluating markets for truly new products and services.

focus groups to figure out customer needs and develop products or services that meet those needs.

Why This Approach to Market Research Is Important to Entrepreneurs

The difference between gathering information about customer preferences for new and existing products and services is particularly important to successful entrepreneurs, who are more likely to develop radically new products or services than to make incremental improvements to existing products or services. Why? Successful entrepreneurs do not have existing products and services on which to make incremental improvements. Therefore, all of their effort to gather information about customer preferences is about preferences for new products and services.

As is explained in greater detail in chapter 6, the best opportunities for you to exploit as a technology entrepreneur are those where a market is new and demand is unknown because the advantages and capabilities of established firms are minimized in these situations. The types of advantages that established firms have—things like having moved up the learning curve and having created capabilities—are least important when a market is new. As a result, you are best off

Stop! Don't Do It!

1. Don't exploit opportunities in which traditional market research techniques are best at gathering information from customers. You won't be able to compete with large, established firms at getting this information.

2. Don't forget that you are just as good as an established company at gathering information about a product or service that no one has heard of before.

introducing new products and services in situations in which the traditional market research techniques of focus groups and surveys are least effective. Moreover, it is in precisely these situations that established firms will often obtain the least accurate information about customer preferences. Because large sample research tends to be inaccurate for uncertain opportunities, the large sample market research techniques of established firms are most likely to lead them astray, thereby giving you an advantage in understanding customer preferences for new products and services.

Absolute Necessities, Nice to Haves, and Things That Are Unnecessary

One of the hardest parts about identifying a real need is distinguishing between things that are absolutely necessary for a customer to have, as opposed to things that are nice to have, and things that are unnecessary to meet customer needs. Most of the time customers provide entrepreneurs with a bunch of information about their preferences, and entrepreneurs need to sort that information into what is necessary, a plus, or unnecessary. Take a hand sanitizer. It is absolutely necessary for it to kill bacteria. If it fails to get rid of the E. coli, it is of no use to anyone. It would be nice to have it cost next to nothing, but that is not actually necessary. Even if it costs a little something, customers would pay for it. What mechanism is used to get the chemicals into the container does not matter to meet customer needs.

An entrepreneur trying to meet the need for a hand sanitizer needs to include something that kills bacteria. It would be nice to have it cost less than soap, and, from the customer perspective, it makes no difference how the entrepreneur gets the chemicals into the container. A successful technology entrepreneur needs to separate out the preferences about product attributes to figure out which ones meet customer needs.

Sometimes, differences in what is necessary, what is nice, and what is unnecessary vary across segments of the market. If that is the case, you might need to segment the market and develop different products for different segments. For example, one segment might indicate that the color of containers for the hand sanitizer does not matter at all. Another one might say that having the right color is absolutely necessary. This difference would suggest segmenting the market into two groups, one for whom the product comes in all black and one for whom the color varies. This segmentation might be crucial if the product would be cheaper in all black containers because offering it that way allows you to offer something that is nice to have—a lower price.

Of course, the information about customer needs that suggests multiple products and segmentation is not all good. You might not be able to launch multiple products simultaneously when you start a company because of the cost of organizing multiple product development and product launch efforts simultaneously. Moreover, each segment alone might be too small to justify the cost of developing a product to serve it alone. So the information about customer needs and identifying which preferences are absolutely necessary to meet might indicate that a business opportunity is not cost effective to pursue.

Figuring Out an Economical Solution

If you figure out that you can create a product or service that meets a real customer need, the next step in the process is to determine whether that product or service can be produced economically. This is a very large hurdle that many entrepreneurs cannot overcome. Clearly, to make money from the introduction of a new product or service, an entrepreneur needs to produce it for less than the cost at which the product or service can be sold. Unfortunately, many entrepreneurs come up with ideas that would be desirable solutions to customer needs, but cannot figure out how to develop those products or services in a way that is profitable. Take space tourism as an example. No entrepreneur has yet figured out how to get people into space at less than the cost that people are willing to spend to go there. As a result, no one has established a space tourism business. To do so would only mean creating a business that loses money.

The process of developing an economical solution to customer needs is tricky because it involves balancing two conflicting ideas. You can only make money with a solution to customer needs in which a profit can be made on some transactions. If each transaction creates a loss, then scaling up to multiple transactions will only create greater losses that will ultimately exhaust your cash. This problem plagued many of the Internet start-ups of the 1990s—the entrepreneurs that founded many of these companies never could figure out business models that allowed them to make money on each transaction. So getting larger just caused them to lose gobs of money.

What makes this tricky is that, in most businesses, the profitability of each transaction is not the same across all levels of sales (as is discussed in greater detail in the next chapter). Many businesses involve economies or scale, increasing returns, or have large setup costs. As a result, many entrepreneurs invariably lose money on the

Stop! Don't Do It!

1. Don't develop a product or service until you have categorized customer preferences into things that are necessary, things that are nice to have, and things that are unnecessary to meet their needs.

2. Don't forget to figure out a way to create your product or service for less than you are going to sell it.

3. Don't believe that you will make money just because you sell a lot; you have to figure out how to make money on at least some transactions.

initial transactions that they make, but find the transactions under-taken at higher volume to be profitable. This observation points out the difficulty of being an entrepreneur. Often, one thinks that it is possible to generate profitable transactions at higher levels of pro-duction, but the ability to make this happen is not always there, and, even when it is, it is often difficult to obtain enough cash to create a business that produces at the volume at which transactions become profitable.

Offering Better Alternatives Than the Competition

The next step in the process of introducing a new product or service is to make sure that no one else has a better alternative than the one that you have developed. Without a better solution than others are offering, you will find it hard to make sales in a competitive market place. As a result, success will not be forthcoming.

Developing a better solution than that offered by competitors is harder than it looks for two reasons. Entrepreneurs often convince themselves that their solutions are better their competitors' when, in fact, that might not be the case. Why? Entrepreneurs need to be overoptimistic to motivate themselves to undertake the difficult process of founding a new firm. This overoptimism makes it difficult for them to look realistically at their own products and services. For this reason, you need to be very careful not to delude yourself when you introduce a new product or service. Rather, you need to engage in a fair and sober evaluation of the strengths and weaknesses of your solution to customer needs to make sure that your solution is, in fact, better than competitors' alternatives.

You are going to have a hard time knowing about alternative solu-tions to customer needs not yet on the market, but coming out in the near future. Often many people are working on the same technologies at the same time, and each one of them is unaware that the others might have a better solution than they do. Take for example, the large number of people who launched Internet grocery delivery businesses around the same time. Obviously, only one of those businesses could turn out to be the best Internet grocery delivery business. However, many of the entrepreneurs who ultimately founded the inferior delivery services did not know that other people were about to found delivery services superior to their offerings.

How do you learn about alternative solutions to customer needs? The best approach is to use your social network to gather information about possible competitors, particularly those not yet in existence, to make sure to find out who might have a competing product or service. Talking to venture capitalists, potential customers, and other people will often provide you with this information. However, talking to these people is not enough. Successful entrepreneurs know that they have to listen carefully to what these people say. Often, these people will give feedback that indicates that there are competitors with better solutions than those that you are offering. If that is the feedback, you are going to have to change your products or services and make them better than competitors' offerings or give up the effort to introduce the new products or services.

Stop! Don't Do It!

1. Don't start a business unless your new product or service is better than those of competitors.

2. Don't convince yourself that your product or service is better than those of competitors when it is not.

3. Don't forget to consider new products or services that other entrepreneurs are about to introduce.

Understanding the Marketing and Selling Processes

To be successful at technology entrepreneurship, you also have to understand how to market and sell new products and services. This knowledge requires you to master two very important concepts: understanding the process of personal selling and understanding the pricing of new products and services.

The Importance of Personal Selling

Much as people like to say, "A good product sells itself," most new products do not sell themselves. Therefore, you have to know how to sell to others if you want to be a successful technology entrepreneur. This is harder said than done because effective personal selling is a skill that is in short supply. Most entrepreneurs come from established firms that can rely on an existing brand name or an advertising system to generate customer interest in its products and services. As a result, when people start new technology companies, they often focus on advertising, distribution, and other aspects of marketing, without realizing that those activities are not the key to making sales when a new venture is first established. In the beginning, successful marketing consists largely of efforts by entrepreneurs to sell their new products or service to potential customers directly.

To sell new products and services effectively, you need to get potential customers interested in the product or service by making them aware that you have a new product or service that will satisfy a need or solve a problem that they have. For example, if you have developed a better type of inventory management software, you can generate customer interest by presenting that software at an industry trade show or by meeting with potential customers.[2]

Next, ask the customer what his or her requirements are for purchasing the product or service. For example, would the customer for the inventory management software that we just described require an interface with back office accounting software? Would the system need to work with Windows XP? By identifying specific customer requirements to make a sale, you can determine what aspects of the product or service will persuade the customer to make the purchase.

After the customer requirements have been identified, you may need to overcome customers' objections to make a sale. Most people do not purchase new products or services without seeking to have some questions answered or posing some challenges that need to be overcome. To close a sale, you must provide a convincing answer to these questions and a response to these challenges, providing enough information and evidence to make the customer comfortable enough to commit to the purchase.[3] For example, if you are selling inventory software you might have to persuade the customer that the software works well with the Windows operating system for them to be willing to purchase the technology.

A vital step is closing the sale. As soon as a customer indicates that he or she would be willing to make a purchase, you need to immediately shift into closing the sale so as not to talk the customer out of the purchase.[4] What does this mean in practical terms? Once the customer has shown that he or she likes the product, or has indicated that it has desirable features, you need to move the conversation toward executing the transaction. Typically this means asking a closing question, which indicates that the customer has already agreed to make a purchase. A good example of a closing question is "Would you like the product in blue or red?" Such a question implies that the only remaining decision for the purchaser is the choice of color and focuses attention on concluding the transaction.

Knowing how to sell is important, but knowing whom to sell to is also important. If you are going to be a successful technology entrepreneur, you need to pay attention to how purchasing decisions are made. Often, the party purchasing a new product is not the end user. As a result, you need to sell the product on different criteria than simply showing that it meets the needs and preferences of the user. Take, for example, new computer software purchases in large companies. In many companies, the decisions about which accounting, word processing, statistics, or inventory management software will be adopted are not made by the users of that software, but by the members of the company information technology department. Because the specific departments using the software are not making the purchasing decision, selling the software on the ease of use to the end user or the fit with existing software may not be as important as selling on price or technical capability. Why? Because these things are appealing to the people in the information technology department making the purchasing decision.

Pricing New Products

You cannot sell your new products or services unless you have set a price for them. Moreover, you will not make money unless the price you charge is greater than the cost of producing the new product or service. While this might sound obvious, it is very difficult to make sure that you price a new technology product or service at more than the cost of producing it. Many new technology products and services include high fixed costs. For example, the variable cost of stamping a compact disk with software is a few pennies per disk, but the fixed cost of producing the software program in the first place can run into the hundreds of millions of dollars. Because you must estimate the volume of your sales to determine if your price is high enough to cover costs when fixed costs are large, you could end up pricing your products at a level that is below cost, at least until you have sold a high volume of the product or service.

Selling technology products and services often involve hidden costs that you need to consider. For example, in many industries firms provide customers with credit to purchase their products or services. Because the cost of providing credit depends on your cost of capital, as well as how long it takes the customer to pay off the loan, calculations of the cost of credit are often fairly complex, and could keep you from estimating this cost accurately.

Another issue that affects the price of high-technology products and services is the environment in which they are introduced. In general, it is difficult to introduce a product at a price that does not fall within the same range as existing products and services that are substitutes for the new product. As a result, you must be aware of possible range of prices for the product or service, and make sure that the possible prices are sufficient to generate positive margins for the business. While you might be able to introduce a new product or service at a higher price than the standard range for products or services in the industry, you need to be aware of several factors that limit your ability to do this successfully. You must truly have a radically new product or service for which customers will not see any alternative as an effective substitute. You must have a plan for lowering the price of the product over time, because otherwise you will not be able to transition to sales to the mainstream of the market later. As the next chapter discusses further, this ability to transition to the mainstream of the market is essential to achieving a significant volume of sales for the new product or service. You must not be operating in an increasing returns business or, as was explained in the previous chapter, you will be placed in an uncompetitive strategic position. You must have a compelling explanation for the customer as to why the new product or service warrants such a high price if, as is often the case, its performance is inferior to existing alternatives.

A final issue in pricing new technology products and services concerns the importance of understanding how customers trade off price and other attributes. When products are not commodities, and therefore differ, some customers are willing to pay a higher price for one product than for another. That price difference can be attributed to the different attributes of the two products. But what is the value of each of the differences between products? This is easy to figure out

Stop! Don't Do It!

1. Don't expect your new product to sell itself.
2. Don't forget to sell.
3. Don't set the wrong price.

if the two products only differ on one dimension. If that is the case, then the difference in price must be a result of the differences on just that one dimension. However, if there are two or more differences between the two products, the value of each of the different attributes is much more difficult to figure out. In the latter case, the price gap is spread across the multiple dimensions of difference, and is often very difficult to allocate to each one of the attributes separately. As a result, it is difficult to know how much each additional feature is worth to customers and then set the price accordingly.

Questions to Ask Yourself

1. Why would customers need the product or service that I am proposing?
2. What is the best way to figure out what customer needs are for the product or service that I plan to introduce?
3. What features (things such as size, weight, durability, etc.) will my product or service have and how do these features meet customer needs?
4. How will I produce my product or service for less than it will sell for?
5. Why does my product or service fit customer needs better than those of competitors?
6. What price should I charge for my new product or service?
7. How will I get customers to buy my product or service?

Summary

This chapter focused on the activities that you, as a technology entrepreneur, need to engage in to identify and satisfy real market needs. You need to identify real customer needs: something that must be solved, often because of a problem that the customer has. You must figure out a way to develop a solution to the need because identification of the need alone, without offering a product or service that meets the need, generates no profit. You need to evaluate customer preferences. For established products and services, this is very easy because entrepreneurs can use surveys and focus groups to identify what customers want. However, when products or services are new, these techniques are often ineffective, and you need to use other mechanisms to identify customer preferences, such as detailed interaction with lead users. You need to ensure that your products and services meet customer needs in an economic manner and in a way that is better than the approach offered by the competition. You need to understand the process of marketing and selling in new companies. You need to understand that marketing in new firms relies very heavily on personal selling by entrepreneurs because new firms do not have brand name recognition, superior distribution channels, or other dimensions of marketing that benefit established firms. Moreover, you need to get the prices right for new products, a difficult task because many of these products have high fixed costs and hidden costs, because of the industry environment and because customers trade off price and product and service attributes.

Now that you understand rule number four of technology entrepreneurship, identify and satisfy real market needs, you now turn to rule number five, understanding customer adoption, which is the subject of the next chapter.

5

UNDERSTANDING CUSTOMER ADOPTION

To create a successful new high-technology company, you need to understand the dynamics of markets for new technology products and services. These dynamics operate according to specific patterns, which influence the ability of entrepreneurs to get customers to adopt their new products and services.

This chapter focuses on some requirements that you need to meet if you are interested in securing customer adoption of your new products and services. You need to understand the likely distribution of adopters of their products and services to target their customer base effectively. You need to follow particular strategies to transition from innovators to the majority of the market. You need to select the right segment of the market on which to focus to transition to the majority of the market. You need to assess the size and growth rate of the markets that you are entering. You need to pay attention to the factors that affect the rate of influence diffusion and substitution of new technology products and services.

Nature of Adopters

While you might understandably be excited when your new business sells a product or service to its first customers, meeting the needs of just a few customers is often not enough for you to be successful as an entrepreneur. To be successful, you need to achieve broad adoption of your new products or services by the mainstream of the market. Without selling to the mainstream of the market, you are not going to be able to obtain sufficient sales volume to take advantage of economies of scale in production and distribution, making your cost structure uncompetitive in many contexts. This problem is particularly severe if you finance your new businesses with venture capital because their cost of capital virtually necessitates the reduction in costs and increase in margins that come from selling to the mainstream of the market.

So, how can you, as a technology entrepreneur, achieve widespread adoption of their new products and services? Basically, you need to understand which customers will adopt products when and what characteristics their products and services must have to gain acceptance from a particular segment of the market. Given the limited resources that most new ventures have, managing the adoption process also means that you will have to focus sequentially on different customer segments. As a result, you will have to know how to target the right initial segment of customers.

Projecting Customer Adoption

The first step in this process lies in understanding patterns of customer adoption of new technology products and services. These adoption patterns are grounded in some basic mathematics. The single most common pattern of new product adoption is a normal distribution, as shown in Figure 5.1. Why? Because most patterns of human behavior are normally distributed, with a small portion of peo-

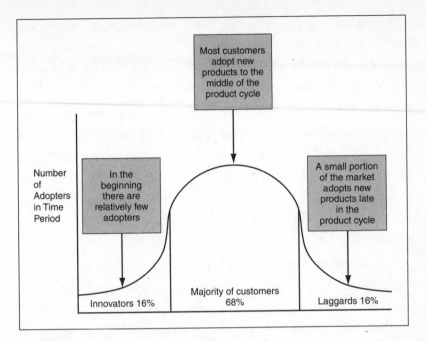

FIGURE 5.1   The Normal Distribution of Product Adoption

ple doing things early, a small portion doing things late, and most people doing things in the middle.[1]

When a new product is introduced, a small number of customers, called innovators, adopt it immediately. This group of adopters is relatively small because new products or services have uncertain value. Most potential customers require a lot of information about the potential value of a new product or service before adopting it, and therefore do not adopt the new product right away. However, a small portion of the market is technologically savvy enough to see the value of new products and services with little information, and so adopts very quickly.[2]

A second group of customers, called the majority, follow the innovators. This group of customers is larger than the initial group of innovators. Why? Because more people are willing to purchase new products and services as information about their value becomes known and their uncertainty declines. The adoption of new technology products and services by the innovators generates information about the value of the new products and services, making it easier for potential customers to obtain the information that they need to make the adoption decision.

Another group of customers, called the laggards, follow the majority. These customers will not adopt a new technology product until it is well established. As a result, this group adopts new products very late in the life cycle. This group is smaller than the majority of the market, generally equal in size to the innovators, because very little of the market is left untapped after the majority has adopted the product or service.[3]

This adoption pattern is probably familiar to you if you have noticed the sales of cell phones over the past 25 years. When cellular phones first came out, they were very expensive, very large, and something that only a few people purchased. But some customers purchased these devices when they first came out, well before most people had even heard of them, let alone purchased them. Later on, the vast majority of the market purchased cellular phones when they became smaller and more affordable. However, even when the majority of customers had purchased their cell phones, some adopters still had not. These laggards purchased their first cell phones only very recently.

Understanding that the typical pattern of adoption of new products and services is normally distributed is important for you, as a technology entrepreneur, for two reasons. It points out that the different groups of customers who adopt new products or services at different points in time often have different motivations. For instance, innovators often purchase new products and services as soon as they come out because they have a need to explore the uses of new technology. These customers are typically price insensitive because there are very few alternatives to the products and services that they purchase, making these products very expensive. (Remember how much the first personal computers cost?) In contrast to the innovators, the majority of customers sees some value in new technology products and services, but requires more information about their value to make the purchasing decisions, and often seeks information about the value of the technology, as well as evidence of successful adoption by other customers, before they are willing to purchase.[4] The laggards are very resistant to new technology and often resist adoption. Often this group adopts products simply because they have no choice due to product replacement.[5]

Understanding that the typical pattern of adoption of new products and services is normally distributed provides a baseline for estimating the proportion of the market that will adopt new technology products and services at each point in time. Moreover, even when adoption patterns do not follow a normal distribution, you can use deviations from the baseline to estimate how different factors influence the adoption pattern.

Capturing the Majority of the Market

An important observation that emerges from the discussion of the distribution of adopters is that innovators do not account for a large volume of business. As a result, you need to figure out how to transition to the majority of the market if you want to be a successful technology entrepreneur.

Unfortunately, most entrepreneurs find it very difficult to transition from sales to innovators to sales to the majority of the market, a situation that led marketing consulting Geoffrey Moore to term the transition "crossing the chasm" (see Figure 5.2).[6] The difficulty of crossing the chasm means that many entrepreneurs do well when they first introduce a product or service to innovators, but then run into trouble when they try to expand to the mainstream of the market.

For you to transition your product or service successfully to the mainstream of the market, you will need very important changes to

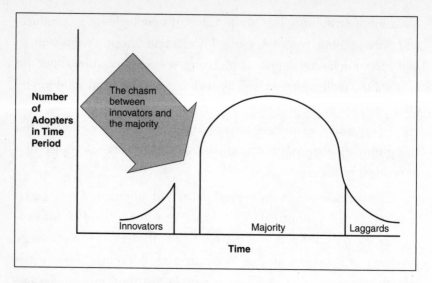

FIGURE 5.2   Crossing the Chasm

your efforts to sell your new product or services to customers. When you transition to selling to the majority of the market, you will suddenly be confronted by customers who demand strong evidence of the value of your products and services instead of facing customers who find all new technology products and services appealing. As a result, you must gather evidence and explain how your new product or service provides greater value to customers than the alternatives offered by competitors.[7]

Moreover, the majority of the market is not as technologically savvy as the innovators, leading them to seek a solution to their problems rather than just a piece of technology. For example, an innovator might buy raw software code and make effective use of it because of his or her technical knowledge. However, the majority of customers need the whole package of things that go with software—a manual, technical troubleshooting help, and so on. As a result, you must package a solution to customer problems to transition successfully to the majority of the market.

You probably will not have the resources to provide packaged solutions to customer problems in all segments of the market simultaneously. Consequently, you will have to concentrate on a single niche of the market when you transition to selling to the majority of the market, lest your resources be spread too thinly across many activities.[8]

Selecting the Right Customers

The idea that you must concentrate on a single market niche at the time when you transition to serving the majority of the market begs the question: which segment should you focus on first? The answer lies in figuring out which customers have the greatest need for your new product or service. You should target market segments that have the greatest need when you transition to the majority of the market because the ability to demonstrate the value of the new product or service to the customer will be greatest for the segment of the market with the greatest need.[9]

This is an important point because many entrepreneurs make the mistake of targeting the market in general, trying to build broad interest, rather than focusing on the customers with the strongest need to buy. Take, for instance, a company with a new home furnace system. That company is much better off targeting the new home builders rather than general homeowners. While some general homeowners might need new furnaces, targeting them is not very effective; only a small percentage of homeowners have a need to buy. It is much more effective for the entrepreneur to focus on the new home builders, who all have a need to buy furnaces.

When is a customer need for a new product or service large? Generally, if the new product or service improves customers' productivity, cuts their costs, or allows them to do something that they otherwise could not do.[10] For example, a taxi company might have a compelling need for a computerized system to track the location of vehicles because that system would allow dispatchers to send the closest taxis to a customer and increase the number of fares handled.

While selecting customers on the basis of who has a compelling reason to purchase seems straightforward, the process is actually pretty difficult. One part of this difficulty lies in the fact that gathering information from existing customers—the innovators—often is not helpful at telling you what you need to know to satisfy the majority and, in fact, frequently leads the entrepreneur astray. Because you need to do things differently when transitioning to the majority, existing customers are not a good source of information; these customers have different needs and preferences from the mainstream of the market.[11]

Another part of this difficulty lies in the fact that you have to estimate the value that comes from your new product or service to appeal to the majority. As was said earlier, the majority of the market tends to make its adoption decision on the basis of value, rather than desire for the newest thing. As a result, these customers demand evidence of the value of new products and services before making their purchasing decisions.

Sometimes it is easy to demonstrate the value of new products and services because that value can be measured easily. For instance, the value of a new product that speeds a customer's assembly line by 25 percent can be measured by simply comparing the speed of the assembly line with and without the new product. Most of the time, however, the value of a new product or service is hard to measure. For example, a new product or service might help a company to avoid losing valuable employees or to improve labor relations. This value is

Stop! Don't Do It!

1. Don't try to transition to the majority of the market without changing how you sell your new product or service.

3. Don't forget to focus on the customers with the most compelling need to buy your product or service when you transition to the mainstream market.

hard to measure in quantitative form. As a result, it will often be difficult for you to persuade the majority of customers that your product or service is worthy of adoption. Nevertheless, you need to quantify the value of these things if you hope to transition to the majority of the market.

Understanding Market Dynamics

Another important aspect of being successful at introducing new products or services lies in understanding market dynamics. Successful technology entrepreneurs recognize the dynamism of markets and understand the evolutionary patterns of growth and development of products and services in these markets. Therefore, they use dynamic strategies to introduce their new products or services. This section introduces some of the key principles of market dynamics that successful entrepreneurs exploit to their advantage.

Markets for all new products and services are initially small. After all, the day before a market is created, its size is zero. Because all markets for new products and services begin at zero and grow from there, estimating the size of the market for a new product or service is not easy. It requires you to engage in a couple of key activities. You must avoid the trap of making static estimates of markets. You must understand the factors that influence the diffusion and substitutions of new products and services.

The Trap of Static Estimates

Unsuccessful entrepreneurs often fall into the trap of trying to estimate the size of a market for a new product or service by thinking about the problem in static terms. The typical unsuccessful entrepreneur follows a process that goes something like this: He or she goes on the Internet or to the library and obtain some demographic information on the size of a market. If the market that the entrepreneur is targeting does not yet exist, he or she selects the closest existing market and uses the size of that market to estimate the size of the target market. For instance, take an entrepreneur who has developed a new communications device called e-mail. At the time that the entrepreneur introduces the first e-mail communications system, no one has a way to send messages from computer to computer. So the entrepreneur estimates the size of the market by looking up how many telephone calls people make each day. Then the entrepreneur estimates the proportion of telephone calls that the new technology—e-mail—will replace, and presto, the entrepreneur has a market size estimate.

What's wrong with this approach to estimating market size? Basically, a couple of things. Static market assessments do not tell you how markets change over time. However, the timing of the growth of a market for a new product or service matters a great deal. Just think about the difference in the sales growth rate of a new company if e-mail becomes a billion-dollar market in five years rather than in 150 years. By failing to measure market size dynamically, you would miss a big part of the market size picture. It isn't just how big the market ultimately will be that matters, but also how fast it gets there. Moreover, the rate of growth over time is not linear. There is an acceleration point that results from the transition from the early adopters to the mainstream of the market. Therefore, failing to examine market growth dynamically makes it difficult to incorporate the effects of timing on patterns of market growth.

Also, using information on the size of an existing market for another product or service to generate an estimate of the size of the market for a new product or service requires you to make an assumption about the substitution of a new product for an old one. For instance, to use information on the telephone market to estimate the market for e-mail, you have to assume that the purpose of e-mail is to *replace* the telephone, making e-mail a substitute for that product, rather than a substitute for regular mail, faxes, face-to-face conversations, or other forms of conversation. If the true purpose of e-mail is to substitute for other products such as regular mail or faxes, then an estimate based on the size of the market for telephone calls is not going to be very accurate.

As we know, e-mail does not just substitute for the telephone; it is also a substitute for face-to-face conversations, mail, and faxes. In addition, e-mail is a complement to telephone communication in many cases, as people often send e-mail messages to clarify telephone calls and vice versa. As a result, by assuming that e-mail substitutes for the telephone in the evaluation of market size, you will likely get a number that has nothing to do with the size of the actual market for e-mail communication.

Moreover, in many cases, like the example just discussed, the estimates are based on the assumption that the new and old products will be substitutes rather than complements. If the products turn out to be complements, then the information about the size of the market for the old product is not very useful as a stand-alone factor in figuring out the demand for the new product. To figure this out, you would also need to know what the relationship was between the demand for the old product and the demand for the new one. That relationship, along with information about the size of the market for the old product, is what is necessary to figure out demand for the new product.

Diffusion and Substitution Patterns

What should you do to estimate market size if the standard static approaches that most people use do not work? The answer lies in looking at adoption and diffusion patterns. Diffusion is the rate at which a new technology product or service becomes adopted by potential users.[12] To correctly estimate market size, you need to estimate how fast a new technology product or service will diffuse. If you can estimate these diffusion patterns accurately, then you can use them to create an accurate picture of market size at different points in time.

An initial step in this process is to go back to the normal distribution that underlies the adoption of most products and services. Successful entrepreneurs know that, if most adopters of new products are normally distributed, then the growth of markets for most new products and services is not linear, but is S-shaped (see Figure 5.3).[13] Why? In the beginning, when only small numbers of innovators purchase new technology products and services, the rate of diffusion is slow. However, when the providers of those new products and services are able to sell to the mainstream of the market, the rate of diffusion accelerates. After the majority of the market is satisfied, the rate of diffusion slows down because the number of laggards in a normally distributed market is smaller than the number of majority customers.

However, all diffusion is not S-shaped because a variety of factors influence the rate of diffusion. Therefore, you need to understand the factors that influence diffusion and consider the impact that they have on the diffusion of the particular product or service that you are

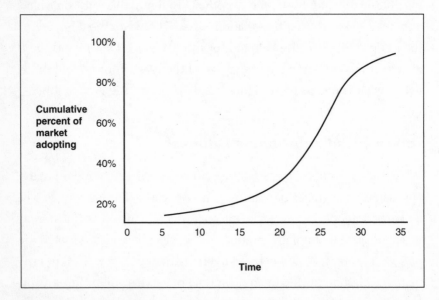

FIGURE 5.3   The S-Shaped Curve of Diffusion

introducing. The nature of the new product or service has an effect on diffusion. For instance, new products or services that are based on discrete technologies—they do not depend on the development of complementary technologies—diffuse faster than systemic technologies because systemic technologies can only diffuse as fast as their slowest diffusing component. Take, for example, the problems that the developers of fuel cells have. Fuels cells generally use hydrogen. As a result, the diffusion of fuel cell vehicles depends on the rate of diffusion of fueling stations to deliver the hydrogen or other inputs to the fuel cells. This is one reason why automakers are working with the oil companies to get them to use gas stations as distributors to provide necessary inputs for fuel cells.

Moreover, products and services based on more costly technologies are slower to diffuse than products or services based on less expensive technologies because people are slower at adopting things that cost more money. Furthermore, products and services that offer greater advantage to users are faster to diffuse than those that offer lesser advantage to users because people's motivation to adopt new products and services increases with the level of advantage that they provide. Finally, new products and services based on easier to understand technologies diffuse faster than those that are based on more difficult to understand technologies because people must understand the value of new products and services to adopt them.[14]

The characteristics of the target market matter. Wealthier people and organizations adopt technology more readily because wealth provides a cushion that facilitates adoption. Similarly, parties that are more financially diversified are more likely to adopt quickly because diversification reduces the risk of adopting new products or services.[15]

However, wealth is not the only attribute of people that influences their willingness to adopt new products and services. Certain types of psychological characteristics among potential adopters, such as tolerance of uncertainty, speed diffusion because they make people more open to the idea of a new product or service. The characteristics of the social structure also influence diffusion. The adoption of new products and services occurs faster in target markets with greater interconnection of potential adopters because such markets have greater levels of communication between adopters and potential adopters, which facilitates the transfer of information from existing adopters necessary for potential adopters to make the adoption decision.[16]

The external environment in which the adoption decision is being made affects the rate of diffusion of new products and services. For instance, new products and services diffuse faster when interest rates are low than when they are high because the cost of obtaining the new product or service is lower when interest rates are lower. Moreover, this effect is larger the more expensive the new product or service tends to be because the use of financing to obtain new products and services increases with their cost.

Political and regulatory factors also influence the rate of diffusion of technology. For example, when an important political group opposes the adoption of a new product or service, diffusion is much slower than when such opposition is absent. Similarly, when regulatory requirements for the adoption of a new product or service are high, adoption tends to occur much more slowly than when regulatory requirements are low.

In some cases, technology diffusion is actually halted by some event or obstacle. Oftentimes, these events or obstacles are political or regulatory. For example, nuclear power was following an S-shaped pattern of adoption as a source of generating power in the United States until the Three Mile Island disaster. That event truncated the diffusion of nuclear power and kept further adoption from occurring.[17]

The diffusion of new products and services is affected by substitution. Substitution use of one technology product or service in place of another technology product or service to achieve the same goal.[18] While some people argue that all new products and services are substitutes for some existing product or service, this substitution is more direct in some cases than in others. For example, fiber optic cable is a substitute for coaxial cable because telecommunications firms use fiber optic cable in the same places that they use coaxial cable.

This mathematical relationship underlying substitution means that the diffusion of the new product or service causes the sales of the old product or service to shrink. Take, for example, the relationship between traditional cameras and digital cameras. Since the mid-1990s, digital camera sales have increased from under a million units per year to almost 10 million units per year. Because the digital camera is a direct substitute for the traditional camera, the sales of traditional cameras have shrunk by an amount comparable to the rise in the sales of digital cameras.

When established firms have large investments in an older technology, substitution is very problematic for them. Take, for example, the voice-over Internet protocol technology. This technology allows people to use the Internet to make telephone calls, making it a substitute for traditional circuit switch technologies. In the telecommunication industry, this type of substitution is a large threat to existing companies because the technological substitution could make obsolete the large investments that traditional phone companies have in circuit switch technologies.

Because substitution makes the investments of established firms obsolete, it is a very important part of the strategy that successful technology entrepreneurs use to compete with established firms. This strategy is particularly valuable in industries that have significant economies of scale. Why? As the new technology substitutes for the old one, the businesses producing products and services based on the old technology suffer from increases in their costs because substitution erodes their scale economies. Often the loss of the advantages of scale economies increases the cost structure of the established firms enough to allow new firms to develop a competitive advantage over established firms.

Of course, making substitution an effective part of your new firm's strategy is more difficult than it looks. One reason is that the pace of substitution is important and varies a great deal across products. For example, it took synthetic rubber 58 years to drive natural rubber down to only 10 percent of the market, but detergent soap took only nine years to push natural soap to a 10 percent market share.[19] As a result, in detergent soap, entrepreneurs introducing the products based on the new technology were able to make strategic use of the rapid deterioration of the cost structure of established firms in ways that entrepreneurs introducing products based on synthetic rubber could not.

Estimating the time to substitution of a new product or service is also an important skill for you to master. As a technology entrepreneur, you need to achieve adoption of your new product or service before you run out of cash. This need creates a balancing act between creating enough supply to meet demand and preclude the entry of competitors, and not creating so much supply that cash is exhausted before demand appears. Take, for example, an entrepreneur who wants to sell a new product or service based on a new technology— say electric motors, which will substitute for a product that is based on an existing technology—say internal combustion engines. The entrepreneur's sales depend on the substitution of the new technology for the old one. If the entrepreneur bets that the substitution of electric vehicles for gasoline powered ones will be slow, he risks not being able to meet demand for the new product or service if that substitution occurs more quickly than he or she anticipated. On the other hand, if the entrepreneur bets that the substitution will be quick, he or she risks running out of cash before the new technology begins to replace the old technology in volume.

Another important concept that you have to consider when you seek to understand substitution is the concept of multilevel substitution. Multilevel substitution is substitution of a product based on one technology for another product based on a second technology, which, in turn, faces substitution by a third product based on a third technology. Steel making provides an example of multilevel substitution. While the open hearth steel making process provided direct substitution for the Bessemer process, the basic oxygen steel making process substituted for both open the hearth steel making process and the electric process.[20] While understanding direct substitution is very straightforward—the new product gains at the expense of the old one—understanding multilevel substitution is much less straightforward. The new product may not substitute at all for one new product or might substitute for the old product, but might itself be completely replaced by a third product before the effects of substitution can be seen.

A final concept that you need to consider in understanding substitution is that the providers of existing products and services that are based on an older technology often take action, political and otherwise, to protect their position and deter change. As a result, products based on new technology do not always diffuse at their natural pace, if at all. For example, producers of glass windshields might take action to keep auto insurers from authorizing repairs to cars made with plastic windshields as a way to deter substitution. Because auto

Stop! Don't Do It!

1. Don't expect a linear rate of adoption of your product or service; it is likely to be S-shaped.

2. Don't use static estimates to evaluate the size of the market for your new product or service.

3. Don't ignore the factors that influence diffusion and substitution in calculating the growth of the market for your new product or service.

Questions to Ask Yourself

1. What adoption pattern do I expect my product or service to follow?
2. Why will innovators buy my product or service?
3. Why will the majority of the market buy my product or service?
4. Why do customers have a compelling reason to buy?
6. How large is the market that I am planning to enter going to be?
7. What will influence how fast my product or service will diffuse?
8. What products and services will my new product or service substitute for?

insurers pay for many of the repairs to automobiles damaged in collisions, this type of action can keep substitution from occurring.

Summary

This chapter focused on explaining customer adoption of new products and services. The first section explained that adopters of new products and services are typically normally distributed because a small proportion of adopters make the adoption decision early and a small proportion make the adoption decision late, while most adopters make the adoption decision in the middle of the process. Important implications for entrepreneurs emerge from this pattern. Different adopters have different preferences, and these preferences influence what you, as a technology entrepreneur, must do to get customers to adopt your new product or service. In addition, the proportion of the market adopting at any point in time is not linear. Rather, it is S-shaped, initially starting small, accelerating, and then declining.

The middle section of the chapter focused on how entrepreneurs transition from innovators to the majority of the market. This transition is important because most entrepreneurs need widespread adoption of their products and services to earn sufficient returns to survive over time, yet most entrepreneurs are unable to navigate this transition. To transition successfully, you, as a technology entrepreneur, must adapt your product or service to the different demands of the majority of customers, provide evidence of the value of the new product or service, and offer a complete package that solves customer problems.

You must also select the right customers to target to transition to the majority of the market. This focus is necessary given the limited resources of new firms. The right set of customers to target is the set for whom the new product or service will increase productivity, cut costs, or provide the ability to do something that they otherwise could not do.

The final section of the chapter focused on explaining market dynamics. The observation that markets are dynamic means that static estimates of markets are not very useful for entrepreneurs. It also means that understanding diffusion and substitution patterns is crucial to their success. Among the important things that you need to understand to be a successful entrepreneur that emerge from this is that the characteristics of the customers, the characteristics of the product or service, the type of substitution, and the timing of the process, all influence the patterns of diffusion and substitution.

Now that you understand rule number five of technology entrepreneurship, understand customer adoption, we now turn to rule number six, exploit established company weaknesses, which is the subject of the next chapter.

6

EXPLOITING ESTABLISHED COMPANY WEAKNESSES

Unfortunately for most entrepreneurs, managers in established companies often pursue the same business opportunities that they do. As a result, a successful entrepreneur not only needs to identify a valuable business opportunity, but he or she needs to out-compete established companies. This is very hard to do. Although most entrepreneurs would not like to admit it, most established companies exist because they are doing a good job. The managers of those companies have identified real customer needs, have come up with valuable solutions to meet those needs, and have developed significant competitive advantages. As a result, most of the time, established companies are at an advantage when entrepreneurs try to compete with them.

So, what should you do? The answer is for you to target the weaknesses of established companies. This chapter explains why it is important for you to target the chinks in the armor of established firms by laying out why established firms succeed almost all of the time when new firms try to compete with them without targeting their weaknesses. Then the chapter identifies the specific weaknesses of established companies, and explains how you can go about exploiting them.

Why Established Companies Win Most of the Time

Established companies are generally better at exploiting business opportunities than new firms for several reasons that have to do with the advantages that firms develop over time: the learning curve, reputation effects, positive cash flow, scale economies, and complementary assets in manufacturing, marketing, and distribution. Let's take a look at why these things place new firms at a disadvantage in competing with established firms.

The Learning Curve

Most of the activities that firms engage in are things that involve some type of learning by doing. While people can learn some things by watching others or by reading about what others have done, most aspects of learning in business are only learned by doing them. Companies learn how to manufacture more efficiently, market more effectively, manage people better, and a host of other things by engaging in those activities. The effect of this learning means that the more times that firms engage in an activity—be that selling, manufacturing, product development, or anything else—the better they get at that activity. This tendency to learn means that most business activities display a learning curve, which is a graphical representation of the relationship between the number of times something has been done and performance at that activity. Take manufacturing products as an example. The more units of a product that a company produces, the more efficient it gets at production.

Why does this learning curve matter to you as a technology entrepreneur? You are very unlikely to start at the same point on the learning curve as an established company with which you are competing. The established company has, through its past operations, moved up the learning curve to a higher point. As a result, as Figure 6.1 shows, new firms are generally worse than established firms at key activities, such as manufacturing and marketing, when they first start, and this makes it difficult for them to compete with established firms.

Reputation Effects

Another advantage that established firms have over new firms is reputation. Selling products and services to customers depends on the reputation of the seller. Customers prefer to buy from companies

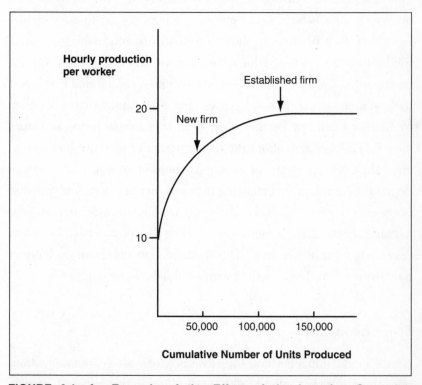

FIGURE 6.1 An Example of the Effect of the Learning Curve on Production Rates

with which they have had a successful transaction in the past or companies that someone they know well, such as a friend or family member, has had a successful transaction with in the past.[1] The reputation that successful past interactions provide make customers inclined toward the seller for transactions in the future. This, of course, is what provides established firms with an advantage over new firms. Established firms have a reputation for successful past transactions, whereas new firms do not. As a result, new firms find it harder to attract customers than established firms, and this added difficulty often makes them uncompetitive with established firms.

Cash Flow

Established businesses, if they are successful, develop positive cash flow. This positive cash flow allows managers to invest in the development of new products and services without having to raise money from investors because it allows them to use internally generated funds. New companies, which have not yet made any sales, cannot have positive cash flow, and so must obtain the capital that they need to develop new products and services from the capital markets, either by issuing equity or by taking on debt. Because external investors have less information about the development of new product or services than entrepreneurs or managers themselves, external investors demand a premium for financing new product development, relative to the cost of using internal cash flow. Therefore, new companies face a financial cost disadvantage in developing new products and services relative to established firms. This financial cost disadvantage hinders new firms when they compete with established companies.

Scale Economies

Established companies have the advantage of scale economies, which help them to produce and sell new products and services at a lower cost than new companies are able to achieve. Whenever the production of a product or service has a high fixed cost for the creation of the first unit, and a relatively low marginal cost of producing additional units, the marginal cost of producing each additional unit is lower than the average cost of producing all of them. Take producing a music CD as an example. The cost of producing the first CD is very high because you need to have a song writer write a song, have a recording artist record it, and set up the facility to produce copies of it. However, once this is all done, it costs only a few cents to make each additional copy of the CD—the cost of burning the recording onto the disk, packaging it, and shipping it. As a result, the average cost per unit of producing 1,000 CDs is much higher than the average cost of producing 10,000 CDs.

What does this have to do with your efforts to found a new technology firm and compete with established companies? Actually, it has a lot to do with it. New firms cannot immediately achieve the level of production of established firms with which they compete immediately upon entry. The risk of such action is often too high to allow them to attract financing, and the management challenges of getting a large operation off the ground are extremely large. Most new firms start smaller than their established competitors, putting them at a cost disadvantage. Moreover, even if new firms could get to large-scale production immediately, they would still have to pay for the fixed cost of getting started. Because the established firm has already paid for this fixed cost and is operating at a higher volume, its cost of producing additional units is much lower than that of a new firm. The end result is that the new firm is not cost competitive with the established firm.

Complementary Assets

Established companies have an advantage over new firms because they already control the complementary assets that are needed to exploit a new product or service. Complementary assets are any assets that need to be used along with an innovative new product or service.[2] For example, suppose you developed a new drug that cures cancer.

The new drug is an innovative product that would meet a customer need. To sell that product to customers, however, you would need a complementary asset—a pharmaceutical sales force. Why? Because drugs are sold through pharmaceutical sales representatives to doctors who can then write prescriptions so that people can obtain the drugs.

An established pharmaceutical company, say Merck, already has a pharmaceutical sales force. Therefore, Merck can deliver the new drug more quickly and effectively than a new firm, which would first have to establish a sales force to exploit the new product or service. It might not be possible to contract with pharmaceutical firms to create a sales force because pharmaceutical firms have no incentive to contract with the entrepreneur, who will be a competitor. And there might not be any companies that serve as independent representatives in the pharmaceutical industry. As a result, the new firm might have to hire a sales force from scratch, a costly and difficult endeavor.

Not only would this effort be very time consuming and slow the ability of the new firm to compete with established firms, but also it might prove very costly. Economies of scope exist in many businesses. For example, pharmaceutical sales representatives sell many different drugs when they call on doctors. A new firm that enters this market with one new drug would not be able to sell as many drugs to customers as its established firm competitors. As a result, it would have a much higher cost of sales than the established firms, which have economies of scope and can sell several drugs at the same time. This higher cost structure might render the new firm uncompetitive.

Established Company Weaknesses That New Firms Can Exploit

What should you do to compete with established firms? The answer is that successful entrepreneurs offset the advantages that established companies have by exploiting the weaknesses of established firms.

Even the best established companies have Achilles' heels by virtue of being established entities. Such things as seeking efficiency, exploiting existing capabilities, listening to customers, exploiting an existing organizational structure, and rewarding people for doing their jobs provide advantages to established companies in many settings, but make it difficult for established companies to compete with entrepreneurs to exploit many opportunities. Successful entrepreneurs exploit these points of weakness by focusing on opportunities in which these things offset the advantages that established firms have over new firms.

The Focus on Efficiency

Established companies often seek greater and greater efficiency in their operations. By becoming more efficient, they can often achieve cost advantages over their competitors. For instance, a company that can manufacture a product at 80 percent the cost of its major competitors might be able to sell its products at lower prices than competitors and steal the competitors' customers. Therefore, efficiency is very important when firms are competing in an industry.

While this focus on efficiency is a basis for the competitive advantage of established firms, it is also an Achilles' heel because it makes it very difficult for established firms to introduce new products and services. The introduction of new products and services often involves some research and development. Research and development is a very inefficient activity because change is uncertain. Every unsuccessful research and development effort results in costs that are not recouped. Therefore, in the effort to achieve efficiency, many firms cut back on their investments in research and development as a way to improve the short-term efficiency in their existing operations. By wringing out inefficiency, established companies often become unable to develop new products and services, opening up a window for new companies to exploit opportunities.

The Exploitation of Existing Capabilities

Established firms are often very effective at exploiting their existing capabilities to produce products or services or to understand markets. After all, they have developed these capabilities through years of trial and error; and these capabilities often provide them with advantages in the market place. These capabilities are beneficial to an established firm when a new product or service is largely an extension of the products that the firm is already producing or is based on a technology that improves an existing process. Under these circumstances, new firms, which lack the same capabilities, cannot compete effectively with established firms. Because established companies often have more money, better advertising, existing distribution assets, information on customer preferences, and a host of other advantages, they can introduce incremental new products and services that do not transform markets or tap new markets more successfully than new firms can. For example, Microsoft has large amounts of data on the previous software purchasing decisions of companies that they can use to refine their new product offerings. As a result, most new software companies find it difficult to compete with Microsoft by introducing products that are related to that company's existing product offerings.

However, the effort of established firms to exploit their existing capabilities makes it difficult for them to introduce truly new products or services that create a transition in the marketplace between one paradigm and another. If a new product or service is created in a way that draws upon a different paradigm for production, organization, or distribution, then established firms face significant weaknesses in being able to exploit it.

When the new product or service is based on products or services that create a transition in the market place, they undermine existing competencies. A new product or service based on a new paradigm demands different skills in production than those necessary to make an existing product or service. For example, the shift from vacuum tubes to integrated circuits in computers destroyed existing competencies because it rendered obsolete the expertise that firms had developed in vacuum tubes.

In particular, the learning curve advantage in manufacturing or marketing that established firms have is eliminated when the process of manufacturing or marketing in the industry is changed to something completely new. Once something new occurs, having done something previously offers no advantage to the established business and may in fact hinder the ability of the established firm to develop the new product or service. Take, for instance, the problems that many book retailers had when the Internet allowed for the creation of online book selling. The established firms' capabilities in book retailing were undermined by the new online paradigm. The efforts of book retailers to use their experience to develop online businesses actually made it harder for them to develop effective products or services because the knowledge that they sought to apply was more of a handicap than an asset in the new paradigm.

Another example of this process is found in drug discovery. The Cohen-Boyer genetic engineering patent changed the basis of drug discovery to one based on molecular biology. Many new biotechnology companies were founded in response to this technological shift because pharmaceutical firms did not have molecular biologists on their staffs. (At the time, most molecular biologists were found in universities.) As a result, university researchers founded companies to exploit this new technology. The pharmaceutical companies lacked the skills necessary to create the new biotechnology products that the start-ups created.

A competence destroying product or service requires firms to cannibalize their revenues from existing products or services. This requirement creates a weakness for existing companies, which are reluctant to cannibalize existing revenue stream. New firms, which have no existing revenue, are not faced with this same constraint. For example, Barnes & Noble had to be willing to sell books to many of its existing customers at the additional cost of setting up an online business to establish book sales over the Internet, whereas Amazon.com did not face the same cannibalization of an existing revenue stream to establish Internet book sales.

Another example of this problem of cannibalization is voice-over Internet protocol. This technology takes voice, converts it to a series of zeros and ones, and sends that information over the Internet. This approach is fundamentally different than traditional phone service, which travels along circuits through wires owned by phone companies. As a result, all of the investment of traditional phone companies in laying and maintaining fiber optic cable and in developing and maintaining switches has to be cannibalized if they adopt voice-over Internet protocol. This makes traditional phone companies reluctant to adopt the newer technology. Because new firms do not yet have fiber optic cable, they do not suffer from this need to cannibalize, and are more willing to embrace voice-over Internet technology.

To maintain their focus on their core activities, established firms create routines that lead them to focus on their existing markets and their existing production technologies. These routines are valuable because they allow companies to become more efficient. By focusing on their knowledge of a particular market or particular production or distribution skills, established companies can select new opportunities in an efficient manner, rather than having to evaluate every opportunity that they come across.

However, this approach becomes a weakness when a new product or service is competence destroying because the new product or service might demand a focus on new markets or the exploitation of new production, distribution, or organizational skills. These routines often lead the dominant firms in an industry to dismiss or reject the value of new products or services when they learn of their existence. For instance, Kodak has had a hard time making the transition to digital camera technology, given its focus on the key capabilities for the production of traditional film. This weakness has opened up a window of opportunity for new firms that were not constrained by existing capabilities in traditional film, allowing them to develop the skills necessary to compete in digital cameras without facing immediate imitation by Kodak.

The Need to Satisfy Existing Customers

Any company needs to satisfy its customers to survive. Keeping customers happy is an important activity for any business. But keeping customers happy also creates a weakness that allows new firms to compete with established firms. When companies create new products, those products are often inferior initially to existing products. Why? It is very hard to get everything completely right the first time a new product is developed. As a result, the new products are not as good as alternatives that are already available. This inferiority causes problems when companies ask their customers their opinions of new products. Often, the customers respond negatively because of the inferiority of the new products relative to existing ones, and tell established firms to focus on incremental improvements in their existing products.[3]

This is where the opportunity for the new firm comes in. There is usually another segment of the market that would find the new product to be useful because that segment is not served effectively by the existing product. New firms can often tap this new segment with the new product or service, largely because established firms have so much trouble doing so. As was mentioned earlier, when established companies develop new products, they often ask their customers what they think of those products. Unfortunately for established firms, their existing customers are not a useful group for providing information about the needs of unserved market segments. Almost all customers are myopic and cannot tell producers about their future needs or the needs of other market segments. Therefore, established firms often decide that there is no market for new products and do not pursue them. This approach creates an opportunity for new companies to come into the market and serve the unsatisfied segments of the market.

The new companies, not being constrained by the views of existing customers, can pursue the unsatisfied segment of the market. Rather than talking to the established company's main customers who are not interested in the new product, they focus on the lead users in the unserved segments of the market. The lead users interact with them and help the founders of the new venture to figure out what would make them adopt the new product.[4]

An example of this process at work is the effort to introduce voice-over Internet telephone service. Most large, established companies that are customers of the traditional phone companies have been reluctant to adopt this new technology because it does not provide them with many of the services that traditional telephone service offers. However, some segments of the market have found that the traditional phone companies cannot provide them with the services that they need anyway—for instance, the ability to leave the same voice mail multiple times without repeating it—and see voice-over Internet protocol as a solution to their problems.[5] These firms have become the initial customers of new companies who enter to provide voice over Internet phone technology.

Once the new company enters the market without response from established firms, it can establish a beachhead to expand to other market segments.[6] Over time, the new company improves the technology underlying its product. That improvement makes the product useful to a wider range of the market, and allows the new firm to expand and take customers away from the established firm that initially accommodated its entry. For example, initially the major integrated steel mills allowed the minimills to enter because they saw the minimills as unable to serve their main customers. The main customers saw the minimill technology as providing too low-quality surface finish for their steel. However, over time, the minimills systematically improved the quality of their steel, and were able to move into the customer base of the integrated steel producers.

The Constraints of Existing Organizational Structure

Established firms suffer from a weakness that comes from having an existing organization structure. All organizations have a structure because that structure allows them to get work done. Most of the time, a firm's organization structure evolves to be appropriate to the tasks of the organization. For instance, a firm that needs a lot of feedback from suppliers in the manufacture of its product typically develops an organization structure that encourages such feedback.

This is where the established firm's weakness comes in. The emergence of a dominant design leads established firms to adopt a particular product design and to cease to invest in alternative designs. Because firms create organizational structures and communication patterns that are appropriate to the production and distribution of products based on these designs, companies tend to fix their organization structure once a dominant design has emerged. Whatever organization structure is adopted creates information filters that are useful for encouraging the exchange of information about the current product design and is problematic for the exchange of information about all other product designs.[7]

When a new product design comes along, the organization structure of established firms filters out information about it. As a result, established firms do not recognize the need for the new design, and new firms often identify that need first. Take, for example, a new design for a vehicle engine that is based on electric power instead of the internal combustion engine. A small number of people at auto companies are experts on electricity. After all, cars do have batteries in them. However, those batteries are not used to run the vehicle's engine. Therefore, the battery people at the auto companies do not interact much with the people designing engine parts. To understand many of the trade-offs necessary to design an electric vehicle, the battery experts need to interact with the engine part people. This lack of interaction makes it hard for people at the auto companies to recognize the right information to design an electric vehicle.

Moreover, even when the established firm's management finally recognizes that a new design is needed, they have a hard time responding to the change because they need to change the organization structure to do so. Take the automobile example we were just discussing. To design an electric vehicle, an auto company has to restructure the organization. Not only do the battery people have to be put in contact with the engine part people, necessitating a restructuring of the organization, but also, the battery people have to be made more important to the organization. Now they are working on something central to the mission of the company. If they rise in prominence in the organization, however, someone else has to fall in importance. And those people will resist the reorganization. Because of these types of issues in restructuring organizations, changing product design is very costly for established organizations. In contrast, new firms do not face the handicap of the old design and so can adopt the new design and the supporting organization structure much more easily and cheaply than established firms.[8]

The Need to Reward People for Doing Their Jobs

To survive, established firms need to reward people for doing their jobs. This process creates two weaknesses for established firms. People typically are not rewarded adequately for developing new products or services in established organizations. In these organizations, people are generally compensated with straight salaries (and perhaps small bonuses) and are expected to perform according to job requirements. To know whether people are doing their jobs, managers monitor employees and compare their performance to target goals. Moreover, established firms must evaluate employees on the basis of nonmarket measures because performance information is diffuse. The division of labor means that individual performance in large firms has little effect on overall performance. As a result, large established firms do not give people adequate incentives to be innovative, and people tend focus their attention on the aspects of their jobs that are rewarded.[9]

Most established companies find it difficult to assign talented people to the development of new products and services. People with the skills to create new products and services prefer to work in new companies where they can have significant upside potential through equity holdings. As a result, established companies often lack the most talented product development personnel. Moreover, established companies make money from their existing operations. This, of course, leads them to assign their most talented staff to those operations, leaving the least talented people to product development work on truly new products.

These weaknesses mean that new firms, which often offer product development people equity, provide stronger incentives for people to develop new products and services. These firms attract the most talented product development people, making new firms better than established firms at most product development activity.

The Difficulty of Product Development in a Bureaucracy

Large established firms often have several other disadvantages that hinder their ability to develop new products and services. Large organizations often lack high-communication density. Because they have many layers of hierarchy, it is difficult for marketing and engineering personnel in large, established firms to collocate and to work together on the product development process, something that a large amount of research has shown is very important in encouraging successful product development.

Large, established organizations often have limited flexibility and offer their employees limited autonomy because they have strong rules and policies to ensure efficiency at ongoing activities. Monitoring requires uniform activities to work effectively. Thus, the monitoring necessary to ensure performance at ongoing operations reduces experimentation and effective product development.[10]

The greater flexibility of new companies allows them to respond to changes in the market or technology much more easily and effectively than large established companies. For instances, biotechnology start-up ARIAD Pharmaceuticals was able to shift from one disease focus, signal transduction, to another, gene therapy, when the founders of the firm figured out that getting to market in signal transduction would take too long. Larger pharmaceutical companies working in the same area could not make this shift because they lacked the flexibility that start-ups, like ARIAD, have.

Moreover, an effective product development strategy involves undertaking opportunity evaluation and action simultaneously, with limited data collection and analysis, and greater use of judgment to make decisions. Established companies often find it difficult to make decisions in this way because the approach conflicts with the goals, policies, procedures, budgets, capabilities, and a host of other things that already exist in the firm. As a result, established firms often make poor decisions about introduction of new products and services.[11]

Stop! Don't Do It!

1. Don't ignore the advantages that established companies have in competing with your new firm.

2. Don't try to go head-to-head with established companies; look for their weaknesses in exploiting new technology products and services.

Opportunities That Favor New Firms

Not only do established firms face weaknesses in exploiting entrepreneurial opportunities that allow entrepreneurs to successfully launch new companies, but also some opportunities are inherently easier than others for new firms to exploit. This section discusses four characteristics of technological opportunities that make them better for new firm formation: discreteness, human-capital intensity, general purposeness, and uncertainty.

Discreteness

New companies perform best when they pursue opportunities to create new products and services that are based on discrete technologies. A discrete technology is one that can be exploited on its own, as opposed to a systemic technology that must be exploited as part of a larger system. For instance, a drug is a discrete technology because it can be administered to patients independently from other technologies. One rarely needs more than a syringe or a capsule to deliver a drug. In contrast, a windshield wiper is an example of a systemic technology because it cannot be used effectively on its own. In the absence of the system that powers a vehicle, a windshield wiper is pretty much useless.

New companies are better off exploiting discrete technologies than systemic ones because of the relative importance of the existing technology to the creation of a new systemic product or service.[12] With a systemic technology, the value generated by the new product can be reaped only if a firm has the entire system in which the new product operates. Established firms will have this system in place, but new firms will need to create it. Because the new firm will need to create the system to reap value from the introduction of the new product, it will gain less from a systemic technology than will an established firm that already has the system in place. In contrast, a discrete technology does not require the re-creation of a system for it to be deployed.

Therefore, established firms have no advantage over new firms in developing products based on these technologies.

Human Capital Intensity

Opportunities that are based in human capital are better for new firms to exploit than opportunities based in physical capital. To understand why, you need to understand the nature of the opportunities that entrepreneurs typically exploit. Three-quarters of the new business opportunities that entrepreneurs discover are related to the businesses of their former employers, either serving the same customers or offering similar products.[13]

This is where human capital comes in. Firms can more easily preclude their employees from taking physical assets that are valuable to the employer and using them to start a new business to serve the same customers as the employer than they can preclude them from taking human capital that is valuable to the employer and using them to start a business. The reason is that our legal system views physical assets as the property of the employer and human assets as the property of the employee. Therefore, it is much easier for an employee to quit his or her job and use his or her human capital to found a company than it is to use the physical capital from where they had been working to found a company. Take, for example, a new business making ski bindings. A company can prevent an employee from quitting and starting a new company to make ski bindings using the employer's equipment. However, the employer is not going to be able to stop the employee from using what is in his or her head—his or her expertise in fitting ski bindings to boots—to start a company to make bindings.

General Purpose

New firms tend to perform better when they exploit general purpose technologies than when they exploit specific purpose technologies. A general purpose technology is a technology that can be applied in multiple markets. A good example is the laser, which is used to make CDs, supermarket scanners, laser pointers, and a host of other products. General purpose technologies are good for new firms because they provide entrepreneurs with flexibility. If one market application proves not to be appropriate for a new technology, the entrepreneur can shift to another market application. This flexibility provides a useful mechanism for helping the entrepreneur manage risk because it minimizes the likelihood that the entrepreneur will invest in something that is sunk and has no value. The flexibility is also useful because it allows the entrepreneur to compare different market applications and identify the most valuable one to pursue. Finally, general purpose technologies are also easier to finance because investors see them as increasing the likelihood that the new venture will come up with a viable product or service.

At the same time, established firms find general purpose technologies difficult to manage. Established firms want technologies that create value in their current markets and at the stage of the value chain at which they operate. Therefore, they can rarely take advantage of the flexibility that general purpose technologies provide, finding themselves constrained by their existing markets and production processes. Focusing on their core businesses, established firms are typically unwilling to invest in the development of general purpose technologies because of the risk that the value will be found in another industry or at another stage in the value chain. As a result, what is valuable about general purpose technologies to new firms is often a hindrance to established firms.

Uncertainty

New firms tend to perform better when exploiting opportunities in new markets with unknown demand. Why? These types of opportunities are ones in which the capabilities of established firms tend to be least beneficial. Large established firms often develop strong

Stop! Don't Do It!

1. Don't start a company to exploit a systemic technology.

2. Don't start a company to exploit a technology opportunity that is based in physical capital belonging to your previous employer.

3. Don't start a company to exploit a single purpose technology.

4. Don't start a company to exploit an opportunity in a market with well-known demand.

expertise in market research based on large sample data collected from surveys and focus groups. New firms cannot easily compete with established firms in using this type of data because they lack the resources and ability to obtain and analyze these data. However, when opportunities are very uncertain because the market is new and

Questions to Ask Yourself

1. What advantages do large established companies have in exploiting the opportunity that I am thinking of pursuing?

2. How can I take advantage large established companies' need for efficiency in exploiting my opportunity?

3. How can I use the focus of large established companies on their existing capabilities to my advantage when I found my firm?

4. How can I take advantage of large established companies' need to focus on their existing customers in building my new business?

5. How can I exploit the disadvantages of the organizational structures and bureaucratic nature of large established firms?

6. How can I take advantage of the way that large established firms reward people when I found my new firm?

7. What dimensions of the technology that I am using favors new firms?

demand is unknown, the large sample market research that established companies are very good at is not very effective. Instead, what works well are small sample efforts to work closely with lead customers. Entrepreneurs can often make decisions on the basis of smaller amounts of information than established firms because they do not need to adhere to large company decision-making rules and norms. As a result, new firms are often better than established firms at making decisions under high amounts of uncertainty.

Summary

This chapter examined how you, as a technology entrepreneur, can exploit established company weaknesses to develop higher performing new technology ventures. The early section of the chapter explained why established companies win competitive battles with new companies most of the time. Established firms have the advantages of having moved farther up the learning curve in manufacturing and marketing, allowing them to produce and distribute new products more efficiently and effectively than new firms. Established firms also benefit from reputation effects. Because they have ongoing relationships with customers, new firms must offer something considerably better than the established firm to attract customers, who have a bias against change. Established firms have the advantage of existing cash flow, which allows them to finance the development of new products and services more cheaply than new firms, which must raise capital from financial markets to undertake this development. Established firms often have the advantage of scale economies, which results from the tendency of new firms to be established at a small scale to minimize risk. Finally, established firms have complementary assets in marketing and manufacturing, which increase the returns from exploiting new products and services.

Although established firms have these advantages, they also suffer from several weaknesses that provide a way for entrepreneurs to compete against them. Established firms focus on efficiency as a way to develop competitive advantages over other existing firms, creating blinders to new product and service opportunities. Their focus is on generating value from existing capabilities, leading them to ignore and discount opportunities where new capabilities need to be created. Established firms need to satisfy their existing customers, and so often neglect opportunities in which new market segments could be targeted with new products and services, and they have existing organizational structures that constrain communication patterns and information flow and so make it difficult for established companies to exploit certain opportunities. Established companies need to reward people for doing their existing jobs, and this constrains them from rewarding people for undertaking innovation. They have hierarchies to manage their existing operations, which inhibits product development.

Opportunities with certain characteristics are also better for new firms to exploit. New firms perform better at exploiting discrete technologies than systemic ones because discrete technologies can be exploited without replicating an existing firm's system of assets. New firms perform better at exploiting opportunities embedded in human rather than physical capital because physical capital cannot be moved as easily as human capital from established firms to new firms. New firms perform better at exploiting general purpose technologies than single purpose technologies because general purpose technologies offer new firms strategic flexibility, which helps them with raising money, with managing risks, and because general purpose technologies often require established companies to invest in markets and production processes that are outside their current capabilities, something that they rarely are willing to do. Finally, new firms perform better with uncertain opportunities because the evaluation of these opportunities demands market research techniques other than the focus group and survey approaches at which large established firms are generally advantaged.

Now that you understand rule number six of technology entrepreneurship, exploit established company weaknesses, we now turn to rule number seven, manage intellectual property effectively, which is the subject of the next chapter.

7

MANAGING INTELLECTUAL PROPERTY

Introducing a product or service that meets a market need is a necessary, but not sufficient, condition for success as a technology entrepreneur. To be successful, you must also protect your innovative new products and services against imitation. Otherwise, you will not capture the returns to your innovative activity, since the profits from introducing new products and services will flow to your competitors.

Unfortunately for technology entrepreneurs, protecting new products or services against imitation is not easy. Most new products and services are simple to copy, particularly for large established firms. Moreover, because established firms have many advantages over new firms—things like an established sales force in place or an efficient manufacturing plant that were the subject of the last chapter—they usually can meet customer needs better than entrepreneurs if they can copy an entrepreneur's product or service successfully. So figuring out how to keep competitors, particularly established firm competitors, from imitating a new product or service is a crucial issue for you.

This chapter:

- Discusses basic ideas behind appropriating the returns to innovation

- Explains why it is so easy for established firms to imitate the entrepreneurs' new products and services, laying the groundwork for understanding why it is important to develop a plan for deterring imitation

- Discusses one of the most important parts of a plan for deterring imitation—the management of secrecy

- Discusses another important part of a plan for deterring imitation—the use of patents as a legal barrier to imitation

Copying Is Easy—And Harmful!

Even though the entrepreneurs who found new firms are often very effective at developing new products and services that meet the needs of customers, they are often very ineffective at capturing the financial returns from introducing these products and services. The reason is that it is usually very easy for others—particularly large established firms—to imitate the new products and services that entrepreneurs have developed. One study by Richard Levin and his colleagues showed that approximately half of the time, the average unpatented new product could be duplicated by between six and 10 competitors at less than half the cost of the original development.[1] Another study, this one by Edwin Mansfield, showed that, on average, one third of new products could be imitated in six months or less.[2]

Established companies find it relatively easy to imitate the new products and services introduced by entrepreneurs for a variety of reasons. Many new products can be reverse engineered, with the technical staff of an established company simply taking apart the entrepreneur's new product and figuring out how it works. Once a company's engineers figure out how another company's product or service works, it is often very easy for them to come up with another way to do exactly the same thing.[3]

Competitors can easily hire the entrepreneur's employees as a way to learn what they know. Labor markets are very free in this country, and people often leave jobs at one company to go work for its competitors. Many companies learn to imitate competitors' products and services by offering a higher salary to their competitors' employees to get them to jump ship. Then they use the knowledge that the employees have to create imitative products and services. While companies can deter this mechanism to some extent by having employees sign noncompete agreements, such agreements are often hard to enforce. Moreover, it is often very hard to prove that employees are using anything more than their general human capital on behalf of their new employer when they help the new employer develop imitative products and services.

Sometimes simply working on similar new products allows competitors to figure out how to copy the entrepreneur's new product or service. Most companies are working on new products and services that are similar to each other, and just knowing that someone else has figured out a way to make a product smaller or add features to it is sometimes enough to allow the company to come up with an imitative product or service on its own.[4]

Competitors can often look at patent disclosures or publications and figure out how to copy an entrepreneur's new product or service.[5] Because engineers and scientists have strong expertise in the area in which they work, they can often extrapolate from partial information obtained in patents or publications and figure out how to imitate a competitor's new product or service just on the basis of information that the competitor makes public.

The ability of competitors to imitate an entrepreneur's product or service is very problematic because imitation will rapidly erode the profits from introducing a new product or service. Say you introduce a new product or service to meet a market need. You may have an initial monopoly because no one else is offering the same product or service to meet that particular market need. This monopoly allows you to charge high prices and reap high profit margins.

Unfortunately, your initial success, if you have any, will motivate competitors to try to imitate the product or service. If competitors can come up with a product or service that meets the same customer need as you are satisfying, they can capture some of the profits that you are earning. To make matters worse for you, the more successful you are at the introduction of the new product or service—and the less you want to be imitated—the easier it is for competitors to imitate what you are doing. Success makes it more obvious that competitors should imitate what you are doing and provides them with the information that they need to imitate your new product or service successfully.

If imitators are not stopped, they will undermine all of your profit. To produce their copies of your initial product or service, imitators need to get access to the same resources as you are using—the employees, the capital, and the raw materials—and bid up their prices, causing your profit margin to fall. Moreover, the imitators take away some of your customers. Each customer that they woo away from you drives down your revenues, adversely affecting your profits.

For you to be a successful entrepreneur, you must figure out a way to capture the returns from introducing new products and services. While the next chapter discusses several mechanisms for doing that, which do not involve deterring imitation, precluding others from copying a new product or service is a big part of what you need to do to be successful. As is explained in more detail, deterring imitation generally involves doing one of two things. Either you must stop the information about how to introduce the new product or service from diffusing out to competitors, or you must create a legal barrier to imitation by other people.[6] You can keep information about a new prod-

Stop! Don't Do It!

1. Don't assume that competitors will have difficulty copying your new product or service.

2. Don't forget to create barriers to imitation of your new product or service.

uct or service from diffusing out to competitors by keeping information secret. You can create a legal barrier to imitation by patenting inventions.[7]

Secrecy

At the most basic level, deterring imitation by reducing the diffusion of information to competitors about how to introduce a new product or service generally involves keeping things secret. For example, suppose you that you have discovered a chemical that makes an excellent fertilizer. If you intend to start a fertilizer company, you might not want to disclose to other people that you have identified this chemical. If competitors and potential competitors do not know that the key to developing your new product lies in the use of a particular chemical, then they will not understand that they need to gain access to that chemical to compete with you successfully. Therefore, they will not seek to obtain access to that resource, and they will not be able to copy your product successfully.

When Does Secrecy Work?

Efforts to mitigate imitation by keeping information about the new product or service secret work best under certain conditions. Secrecy works better when there are few sources of the information about the new product or service other than the entrepreneur. To imitate your product or service, a competitor needs access to the information that makes creation of the copy possible. While the competitors can obtain this information from you, they can also gain it from third parties. The effectiveness of your efforts to keep things secret is not going to be very high if third parties readily provide that information. This is why it is often easier for Coca-Cola to keep other companies from copying its soft drink formula than it is for your local dry cleaner to keep its dry cleaning formula secret. Even if your local dry cleaner never told anyone the formula for its dry cleaning solution, you could obtain it from any of thousands of other dry cleaners. However, if the executives at Coca-Cola do not tell you the formula to classic Coke, you are going to have no way of knowing what it is.

Secrecy is more effective when the new product or service is complex. Imitation involves understanding how to copy a new product or service, not just having access to formulas or blueprints. The more complex a product or service is, the harder it is for people to duplicate it. Complexity affects people's understanding of the order in which tasks need to be undertaken and the difficulty of choreographing the joint efforts of different people, making it harder to duplicate products and services. Take, for example, the difficulty of assembling a child's toy. Even if you have the instructions, it is much harder to reproduce the product just as the manufacturer had intended when the product is made up of hundreds of pieces than when it is made up of only a couple of pieces.

Secrecy is more effective when the process of creating a new product or service is poorly understood. To imitate your activities, people have to understand what you are doing. The fewer competitors that can actually understand what you are doing, the less that imitation will occur. For example, suppose that you developed a new method for keeping storm drains clean by flushing them with a chemical mixture at certain temperatures. The problems that many home owners have with clogged storm drains and the water damage that they cause would lead to a significant demand for a reasonably priced chemical cleaning mixture. Once potential customers knew about the solution, competitors would crop up, seeing the opportunity to make a profit off of the delivery of this cleaning service.

However, what if the process of creating this new chemical solution was poorly understood? That is, for the product to work, very precise amounts of the chemicals have to be combined at exactly the right moments under the right temperature. As long as the process of combining the chemicals was hard to for people to understand, few people would be able to imitate this product, and you would capture the profits from providing this product.

Secrecy works best when the information that is being kept secret involves tacit knowledge, or knowledge about how to do something that is not documented in written form. Good examples of tacit knowledge are a plant manager's knowledge of how to keep an assembly line running a high speed through a sense of where to position different workers with different skills, or a salesperson's knowledge of how to close sales by timing the introduction of personal comments into a discussion.

Imitation is slower when the key knowledge necessary to introduce the product or service is tacit because the ability to write things down in documented form means that the process is either well enough understood or sufficiently simple to express in a step-by-step written form.

If you do not write down the formula for developing a new product or service, then competitors will find it more difficult to figure out the processes that you use to produce and distribute a product or service.[8] Unable to get inside your head, competitors will find it difficult to understand what you know, making it hard for them to imitate your product or service. For example, suppose that you have developed a better process for manufacturing steel, which you keep in your head. Without understanding exactly how you make the steel, it would be hard for your competitors to develop steel using the same process.

Moreover, it is easier to imitate a documented process than a tacit one because imitation of a documented process only requires access to the document outlining the process, whereas imitation of a tacitly understood process requires access to the person who holds that information in their head. Most of the time, it is easier to gain control of a document about a process than to gain control of a person who has that knowledge. Take, for example, the case of expertise in boiler repair. If that knowledge is held in documentary form by a company in Michigan, then a company in Ohio could get control of that information and move it to Ohio more easily than it could if the knowledge was tacit and held in the minds of the Michigan firm's employees. In the latter case, the competitors would need to hire the employees of the Michigan firm and get them to move to Ohio to imitate the product or service.

Secrecy works better when there are limited numbers of people capable of understanding the information. The fewer people that have the skills and abilities to develop the same new product or service as you have developed, the fewer people that can figure out how to imitate what you are doing, even if you keep your knowledge secret. Researchers Lynne Zucker and Michael Darby at the UCLA business school have shown this to be true for new biotechnology companies. They learned that the new biotechnology firms that were founded to exploit the scientific expertise of leading scientists often were successful because competition was limited to the handful of people who also had the skills to exploit the cutting edge scientific techniques that they used.[9]

Trade Secrets

Trade secrecy is a special case of all efforts to keep a new product or service secret. A trade secret is a nonpatented piece of intellectual property that provides a competitive advantage. For example, a new process for refining petroleum or making drugs might be the type of thing that is a trade secret. Other examples might include manufacturing processes, lists of customers, and food recipes. Because trade secrecy is an important special case of keeping information secret, it is useful to go through some of the key conditions for making something a trade secret.

You must take significant steps to ensure that you keep information secret. That means that you must ensure that all employees have signed nondisclosure agreements that are crafted by lawyers who know the details of employment law. After all, information cannot be kept secret, and a case cannot be made that you are trying to keep information secret, unless your employees are expected to refrain from disclosing information.

In addition, you must take active steps to ensure that people do not gain access to the secret information by accident. This means that your company must adopt certain "secrecy policies." Access to the key information must be limited to only those personnel who need it. So, for instance, only three people at Coca-Cola have access to the formula for classic Coke, which is that company's major trade secret. This limited distribution of the formula helps to keep it from getting out. Furthermore, physical access to the locations that contain the secret information must be made difficult. This means that your company facilities must have areas that are off limits to visitors, and plant visits by customers and suppliers cannot include access to these areas.

You must be vigilant to ensure that there are not other mechanisms available to competitors to independently gain access to the information that provides the trade secret. Nothing precludes competitors from using information that they gathered independently (as long as it is through legal means) about any product or service that you develop. So, if you invented a new type of fertilizer that accelerates the growth of grass by 50 percent and a competitor independently discovers the formula through legal means—reading your publications, talking to your suppliers or customers, reverse engineering your product—nothing would stop them from making and

Stop! Don't Do It!

1. Don't use secrecy to protect your new product or service without taking the necessary legal steps to ensure secrecy.

2. Don't use secrecy to protect your new product or service when there are many sources of the information about the new product or service other than you, when the new product or service is simple to create, when the mechanisms to create are well understood, when the key knowledge to create the new product or service is well codified, and when there are many people who could develop your new product or service.

selling exactly the same fertilizer as you provide. Therefore, production processes make better trade secrets than products. Because you sell your product in the marketplace, it will be harder for you to keep its composition secret, than it will be for you to keep secret the production processes used to make the product.

To stop competitors from imitating something you have sought to protect as a trade secret, not only do you need to take efforts to keep it secret and keep competitors from developing the same product or service independently, but you also need to demonstrate that you have a competitive advantage that will be lost if competitors can make use of your trade secret. This means that you must be able to document that what you term a trade secret is central to how your company derives its value, providing an advantage over competition in the marketplace.

Patenting

Most of the time it is virtually impossible to keep secret information about how to produce a new technology product or service. Under these circumstances, entrepreneurs can capture the returns to developing new products and services by creating a legal barrier to imitation by competitors. While there are several legal barriers to imitation—copyrights, trademarks, and patents—patents are really the only ones that have much of an effect at deterring imitation. Therefore, successful entrepreneurs might obtain copyrights and trademarks, but their strategy of using legal barriers to imitation revolves around patents.

A patent is a government-granted monopoly that precludes others from using an invention to create a product or service for 20 years in return for the inventor's disclosure about how the invention operates. To receive a patent, you must have an invention that the patent office deems to be novel. It cannot be an obvious next step in technological development to a person who is an expert in the field, and it must have some commercial usefulness. Moreover, the invention must not have been disclosed publicly either in an open forum or in print, and it cannot have already been offered for sale.[10]

Strong patents are especially important to entrepreneurs, because new firms often lack other forms of competitive advantage when they are first established. Absent better manufacturing or marketing than established firms, which are hard to have when a company is first created, strong patents allow you to create the value chain for your new business before its new product or service is imitated by other firms. The stronger the patent and the broader its scope, the more competitor firms you can deter from imitating your new product or service, enhancing the likelihood that you can put the new company and its value chain in place before imitation occurs.

Moreover, strong patents are extremely important to raising money in industries in which patents tend to be quite effective, such as biotechnology. Because patents tend to be very strong in biotechnology, they are important to raising money. Patents provide a verifiable source of competitive advantage for the new company, which facilitates the process of obtaining financing. They also provide a salable asset if the venture fails. Because investors can "take the patents to the bank" at the end of the day, entrepreneurs are able to raise more money than they can if they do not have such salable assets underlying their ventures.

While patenting provides a very valuable form of protection against imitation for a technology entrepreneur, it does have several limitations. So you should not think that you can simply patent your products and services and your troubles with potential imitation will be over.

One limitation of patenting is that only a plant, process, machine, manufacture, formula, design, or piece of software is patentable. An idea cannot be patented, hindering the ability to patent most services.[11] For example, you cannot patent the concept of courteous service, which is a problem if your strategy to garner value relies on providing better service rather than taking advantage of the components of your product itself.

Moreover, the effectiveness of business methods patents, which allow some ability to protect services, are largely unproven. While you can now patent "business methods," like the "one click" system that Amazon.com uses to allow customers to avoid reentering information in online purchases, a limited history of these patents makes it hard to tell how the courts will interpret their usefulness in precluding imitation of business methods.[12]

Another limitation of patenting is that, to obtain a patent, you need to show how the product or service being patented differs from existing prior art, or previously patented inventions. A patent is only given to a piece of technology that makes an improvement upon a previous invention; if the new technology is an exact imitation of the previous technology, it is not patentable. Moreover, when the invention builds upon previous inventions, a patent on the new invention needs to cite the previous patents. These citations limit the inventor's property right to only those things not claimed in previously cited patents. Therefore, one of the most important aspects of patenting is making the strong claims about exactly what was invented.

The broader the claims on a patent, the better the protection offered by the patent because a patent provides a property right only to what is claimed. When a claim is very narrow, it is easier for other firms to make small changes to the invention and work around the claim. As a result, a claim for a process for mixing chemicals is more valuable than a claim for a process for mixing ammonia because the former protects you against the imitation of all processes to mix chemicals, whereas the latter protects you only against imitation of processes to mix ammonia.

How do you know if a patent has strong claims? You need to look at the patent and see if part of the claims could be changed or dropped and still yield the same invention. For example, if a patent claims the process for using a particular adhesive for attaching two pieces of metal, but you could easily attach the two pieces of metal with another adhesive, the patent has weak claims. All a competitor has to do to get around the adhesive patent is to substitute a different adhesive for the one that you have claimed.

Take, for example, U.S. Patent 6,622,077, which is for an antilock braking system. This patent's first claim is for

an anti-lock breaking system for a wheeled vehicle having at least two axles, wheel-speed sensors and at least one modulator per axle for the adjustment of braking pressures, comprising an electronic control unit having four channels and four end stages, at least one axle of said at least two axles having a single one of said at least one modulator per axle for common control of the wheels on said at least one axle, said single one of said at least one modulator being commonly actuated by two end stages of the four end stages of said electronic control unit, and a coupler to couple the single one of said at least one modulator to said electronic control unit.

This patent claim is strong from the point of view of the type of vehicles in which the antilock breaking systems would be protected. The patent does not just protect an antilock breaking system in a car or a truck, but instead protects an antilock breaking system in any "wheeled vehicle having at least two axles, wheel-speed sensors and at least one modulator per axle for the adjustment of breaking speed." This set of vehicles is pretty broad and offers the patent holder fairly broad protection.

However, this patent claim is not as strong when considered from the point of view of the type of characteristics that the vehicles have to have for the antilock breaking system to be protected. The patent protects only antilock breaking systems in those vehicles that have wheel speed sensors and at least one modulator per axle, which is more limiting than "all vehicles." Moreover, the patent cites a previous patent for a "diagnostic mode selector system for anti-lock brake systems and other electronic systems." As a result, patent 6,622,077 does not cover the property right for the diagnostic mode selector system for antilock breaking systems.

Still another limitation of patents is that they are often ineffective unless you obtain multiple patents, rather than just one. While multiple patents ensure broad claims and provide a picket fence of protection around the product or service, they are more expensive and more difficult to obtain than a single patent. Not all aspects of a patent meet the criteria of novelty, nonobviousness, and value necessary to obtain a patent. Moreover, patents are only as strong as their claims and obtaining multiple patents with strong claims is very difficult.

Take, for example, the start-up of Ronald Demon, an MIT student who invented a shoe that adjusts cushioning to what the user is doing. To keep shoe companies from imitating his new shoe, he has sought patent protection. However, he cannot obtain patent protection on his whole shoe because few of the dimensions of his shoe are novel, nonobvious, and valuable, the criteria for patent protection. As a result, he can only patent specific parts of his new shoe. Because

shoe companies could work around any one of these patents by finding a different way to accomplish the same goal, he needs multiple
patents, each protecting different dimensions of the shoe to ensure
that his new shoe is not copied.[13]

Patents are also expensive. Including all of the filing and legal
fees, a standard patent costs about $15,000. But this is not all of the
costs of patenting. Because patent protection only exists in those
countries where patents are granted, this initial cost has to be multi-
plied by the number of countries in which patent protection is
sought. It really does you no good to just patent your inventions in the
United States if you have any intention of selling your product over-
seas. Imitators can legally imitate an invention by reading the patent
disclosure in the United States and then applying the invention in any
country where the inventor did not obtain patent protection. Because
you must disclose how an invention works to obtain a patent, filing for
a U.S. patent actually teaches people in other countries how to create
the product or service on which the patent is based, and makes it easier for them to introduce the same product or service in their countries. Therefore, if you do not want European, Canadian, or Japanese
firms to imitate your products in their home countries, you would be
facing approximately $60,000 in costs to obtain just one patent.

Moreover, the patent system is not the same across all countries,
adding more expense to the process. At the most fundamental level,
the United States awards patents to the first person to invent a new
technology, whereas countries whose legal systems are based on
Roman Code Law award patents to the first party to file the invention. Therefore, if you, as an entrepreneur from the United States,
seek to obtain a patent in a Latin American country, where almost all
of the patent systems are based on Roman Code Law, you will need
to incur the added expense of seeking to file rapidly, before another
party learns of the invention and preempts your filing.

Add all of this to the fact that a product or service might require
more than one patent to protect it against imitation, and the price

easily escalates to over $100,000 for a new product. Of course, this is only the initial part of the cost. You still need to hire attorneys to defend the product or service against imitation through lawsuits in patent court because lawsuits are the mechanism for enforcing patent rights.

The costs of defending a patent are not trivial. To defend a patented invention against infringement, your lawyers will need to show that an imitator violated the patent's claims and that you suffered damages as a result. This legal process can raise the costs of patent protection into the millions of dollars.

Established company imitators know how costly it is for entrepreneurs to enforce their patent protection and often test entrepreneurs' willingness to defend their patents. As a result, they often imitate patented inventions and run the risk that ultimately they will have to pay damages. While imitators who are found to have infringed a patent have to pay triple damages, established company managers realize that many entrepreneurs will have to give up before a lawsuit reaches that point. Many entrepreneurs simply run out of cash or energy before they can prevail in the several year process of enforcing a patent. As a result, many of them settle for much less than triple damages or give up fighting more deep-pocketed competitors.

Patents are not always strong enough to prevent imitation. In some cases, the scope of the claim you can get is too narrow to offer much protection. As was described earlier, patents are only as strong as their claims and sometimes the good claims have already been given away, leaving you with protection against imitation of only a very limited set of things.

In other cases, it is easy for imitators to invent around your patent and accomplish the same goal as you have achieved without violating the claims of the invention. Inventing around is the process of coming up with something that accomplishes the same goal as the patented invention without violating the claims of the patent. It is possible to invent around patents because there are usually multiple ways of accomplishing the same technical goal. For example, an imitator can often invent around an electronic device patent by changing the design of the circuitry, making the imitative product work the same way as the patented one, but without using the same circuitry design as the patented invention.

TiVo's efforts to enforce a patent on how digital video is saved on a hard disk, against EchoStar Communications, which offers the DISH Network, is a case in point. TiVo claims that the DISH violates its patent because it, too, saves digital video on a hard disk. However, if the DISH stores digital video in a different way from TiVo, accomplishing the same goal through alternative technical means, TiVo's patent will not cover EchoStar's product.[14]

In still other cases, it may be too hard for you to prove that others have infringed your patent or too costly to defend the patent in a lawsuit. It is one thing to think that someone has violated your patent, and it is another to prove it in court. Sometimes technology entrepreneurs cannot amass the evidence that it takes to prove that infringement actually occurred. Other times the fixed costs of defending a patent are so high that it simply does not pay to go through the effort to defend the patent through the court system.[15]

In another set of cases, the technology is developing so quickly in such a wide variety of ways that when patents issue, all of the inventors have overlapping claims that require them to strike licensing deals with each other that undermine the advantage of holding a patent. Given the relatively fixed costs of patents, the potential value generated by them is sometimes too small to justify the cost of enforcing them.[16]

Obtaining a patent requires you to disclose how the invention works. This disclosure obviously makes it easier for imitators to copy your product or service. While you receive a 20-year monopoly in return for this disclosure, sometimes that monopoly is not worth the cost of disclosing. Perhaps the most famous example of this choice is the chemical formula for Coca-Cola which was never patented. Had the formula been patented, the monopoly would have expired long ago, allowing competitors to produce soft drinks with exactly the same chemical composition (and taste!) as Coke. The fact that this formula was never patented is what makes it possible for Coca-Cola to keep from imitators creating exactly the same product as Coke.

A final disadvantage of patents is that they are not very effective in many industries. In general, patents tend to work well in industries in which the core technology is biological or chemical and much worse in industries in which the core technology is mechanical or electrical.[17] The reason has to do with the ability to accomplish the same goals through alternative technical approaches. In things that are biological or chemical, it is hard to make slight modification to the design and yet accomplish the same goal; this is not true for mechanical or electrical devices. For instance, a drug has a very precise molecular structure, and slight alternations could transform the drug from something beneficial to something harmful. In contrast, most electrical devices can be structured quite differently and still accomplish the same goals.

Several researchers have investigated the differences across industries in the effectiveness of patents. Table 7.1 provides some data adapted from the Yale Survey on Innovation, a study that examined the effectiveness of patents across industries by surveying over 600 research and development managers in over 130 lines of business about the effectiveness of patents in their industry. The table shows that in industries like drugs and chemicals, patents are very effective

Stop! Don't Do It!

1. Don't assume that patents will protect your new product or service. Evaluate whether they will work in your situation.

2. Don't forget to compare the effectiveness of patents and trade secrets as a way to protect your new product or service. Trade secrets may be better than patents in your case.

TABLE 7.1 Effectiveness of Product Patents by Industry.

Industry	Effectiveness (7-point scale with 7 equals "very effective")
Drugs	6.5
Organic chemicals	6.1
Inorganic chemicals	5.2
Steel mill products	5.1
Plastic products	4.9
Medical devices	4.7
Motor vehicle parts	4.5
Semiconductors	4.5
Pumps and pumping equipment	4.4
Cosmetics	4.1
Measuring devices	3.9
Aircraft and parts	3.8
Communications equipment	3.6
Motors, generators and controls	3.5
Computers	3.4
Pulp, paper and paperboard	3.3

Questions to Ask Yourself

1. How easy would it be for competitors to copy my product or service?
2. Could my product or service be protected by secrecy?
3. What do I need to do to protect my product or service as a trade secret?
4. Is my product or service patentable?
5. How effective would a patent on my product or service be?
6. What do I need to do to protect my product or service with a patent?
7. Would I be better off with a patent or a trade secret?

at protecting new products, but that in industries like motors and generators or computers, they are not very effective at all.[18]

Summary

This chapter explained that most new products and services are easy to imitate, particularly by large established companies. Companies can often reverse engineer the new products of their competitors to find out how they work and duplicate their functionality. They can also hire the employees of the innovating company to gather tacit knowledge of how the innovator developed the new product or service. They can often look at patent documents, published papers, or other written sources to gather codified information that allows them to imitate the new products or services introduced by entrepreneurs. Finally, established companies can often imitate the new products and services that entrepreneurs develop simply because they are working on similar projects, and their own research and development provides them with needed information to imitate.

The fact that other companies, particularly large established ones with better manufacturing and marketing capabilities than start-ups, can imitate their new products and services is problematic for you, as a technology entrepreneur, because the profits that you earn from introducing a new product or service are eroded by imitation. Therefore, to be successful, you must make concerted efforts to minimize imitation through two alternative means: secrecy and patenting.

Secrecy is a process by which you maintain your unique ability to generate a new product or service by not allowing other people to gain access to the information about how to create the new product or service. Secrecy is most effective as a strategy under several conditions. There are few alternative sources of information other than the entrepreneur to learn how to create the new product or service.

The product or service is complex. There are limited numbers of people who could make use of information about the creation of the new product or service in such a way as to be able to replicate it. The knowledge necessary to create the product or service is tacit. The process by which the product or service created is poorly understood.

An alternative to secrecy available to you is patenting. A patent is a government monopoly that precludes others from making a duplicative invention for 20 years in return for disclosure about how the invention works. Patenting is an important tool for you, as a technology entrepreneur, to use because it allows you to create a new company and assemble the value chain necessary to produce and distribute your new product before competitors can imitate it.

While patents are valuable for deterring imitation, they have several limitations. Patenting is only possible for a small number of types of products or services. To obtain a patent that has strong enough claims to deter imitation, you have to demonstrate that the new product is a significant improvement over prior art. Multiple patents are often needed to protect a single product. Patenting is expensive, particularly given the need to seek multiple patents to protect a given product and the need to seek patent protection in multiple geographic locations. Patents are not always very strong, particularly when the claims are limited by prior art. Patents require disclosure of the invention, which may prove to be more costly to you than the offsetting benefit of monopoly protection. Patents are not very effective in many industries, particularly those based on mechanical or electrical technology.

Now that you understand rule number seven of technology entrepreneurship, manage intellectual property effectively, we now turn to rule number eight, appropriate the returns to innovation, which is the subject of the next chapter.

8

APPROPRIATING THE RETURNS TO INNOVATION

While obtaining patents and maintaining secrecy are important ways that you can capture the returns from introducing new products and services, they are not the only ways to do it. Other mechanisms include learning curves, lead time, first mover advantages, and complementary assets. Although many of these other mechanisms to appropriate the returns from introducing new products and services work better for large established firms than they do for entrepreneurs, you need to be aware of the range of alternatives available. Many types of new products and services cannot be protected by patents or trade secrets. For instance, you might come up with a snowboard binding design and may be unable to patent that design or protect it as a trade secret.

Moreover, mechanisms such as learning curves, lead time, first mover advantages, and complementary assets are all more effective than patents at capturing the returns to introducing new products and services.[1] In fact, research shows that patents successfully capture the returns to new product introduction only about a third of the time, whereas complementary assets in manufacturing and marketing capture the returns to new product introduction over 43 percent of the time, and lead time works over half the time.[2]

This chapter discusses several ways to capture the returns to introducing new products and services, including obtaining control over resources, establishing a reputation, exploiting learning curves, becoming a first mover, and exploiting complementary assets in manufacturing, marketing, and distribution. Each of the sections discusses the conditions under which one of these approaches is effective.

Obtaining Control over Resources

You can appropriate the returns to introducing your new product or service by obtaining control over the resources needed to create the product or service.[3] Suppose, for example, that you want to go into the business of smelting aluminum. Because aluminum smelting depends on access to bauxite, which can be obtained in only certain mines, you might seek to obtain control over the mines that produce bauxite.

How can you obtain control over resources, such as bauxite? You could buy up all of the sources of supply. If you purchased all of the bauxite mines in the world, then no one else could gain access to the bauxite necessary to make aluminum. Of course, in many cases, such as this one, the acquisition approach to obtaining control over resources is very costly. Bauxite mines do not come cheap. An alternative approach would be to obtain control through contracting. For instance, you could sign a contract with all of the bauxite mines to buy up their bauxite. By contracting for the bauxite, you could keep others from gaining access to this source of supply, and so prevent them from capturing the returns from this opportunity.

The key to this strategy is to identify the key sources of supply for the production of the new product or service. While you could capture the returns to introducing a new product or service by obtaining control over any source of supply, some inputs are better targets for control than others. If the input is easily substituted for, then this strategy will not work well. For instance, suppose you did not seek to obtain control over the key sources of bauxite, but, instead, sought to obtain control over the key sources of transporting bauxite to the smelter—trucks. Because other companies could substitute railway cars for trucks, they could easily get around your strategy, thereby undermining its effectiveness.

The strategy also will not work very well if you do not target the bottleneck points in the supply chain. Every product or service involves multiple inputs, some of which are provided by more suppliers than others. Obtaining control over resources is a more effective strategy when the resource that is sought is a bottleneck in the supply chain. Why? Because the bottleneck stage is the one where it is easiest to get control over inputs to the production process. Take our aluminum smelting example again. It would be a foolish idea for you to try to obtain control over the source of supply of screws as a way to capture the returns to aluminum smelting. While screws are certainly an input into aluminum smelting, and you probably cannot substitute for them, the number of possible suppliers of screws is so large that buying them up or even contracting with them is too large a task for a new firm to undertake successfully.

Stop! Don't Do It!

1. Don't try to control resources that can be easily substituted for as a way to appropriate the returns to the introduction of your product or service.

2. Don't try to control resources as a way to appropriate the returns to the introduction of your product or service unless the resources are bottlenecks in the value chain.

Establishing a Reputation

Another way that you can capture the returns to introducing new products and services is by creating a reputation for providing customers with the best products and services. When you create a positive brand name, you are able to generate perceptions in the minds of customers that your product or service is better than those offered by competitors, thereby mitigating the tendency for customers to shift to competitors' products or services even if customers can obtain those products or services at a lower price.

The stronger the perception that other products or services are not worthy substitutes you create in the minds of customers, the more you can capture the returns to introducing new products or services. The stronger the perception, the harder it will be for imitators to attract customers away from you. For example, suppose you developed a new, more energy efficient steam boiler. Other companies may also be able to develop energy-efficient steam boilers. However, if you can convince people that your company is better than competitors at providing those boilers, then the customers will not switch to other providers of boilers, even if the other parties offer their boilers at a lower price.

For you to use a brand-name reputation to capture the returns to the introduction of a new product or service, you usually have to invest in its creation. This investment in brand-name development can be small, and the brand name can develop slowly through word of mouth. Alternatively, you can make a large investment and try to develop the brand name more quickly. This larger investment generally involves putting money into advertising, which provides information to customers about the qualities of the new product or service, and persuades them that these qualities make the product or service better than those offered by competitors.

Advertising is subject to key conditions that make the effort to build a brand name for a new company expensive, and make this type of mechanism a rare one for entrepreneurs (as opposed to large, established companies) to use to capture the returns to introducing new products. Advertising is subject to considerable economies of scale. Most advertising has a high fixed cost relative to its marginal cost—the price of developing and then running a radio, television, or print advertisement tends to be a flat amount regardless of how many units you produce. As a result, advertising is very expensive on a per unit basis when a company first starts and is producing very few units of its product or service. Of course, later, the advertising cost per unit falls as production volume increases.

It takes a long time to build a brand-name reputation through advertising. The nature of the human mind is such that it can only process a certain amount of information at a time, whether that is from advertising or some other source. As a result, people do not absorb much about each ad every time they see it. For advertising to be truly effective, it requires repeated messages over a long period of time. This means that you have to invest in advertising for a while before you can see the benefits of that investment.

The effect of economies of scale and the slow process of persuading people of the value of something mean that you have to obtain very large amounts of capital to use advertising to build the brand name of a company that you start. It also means that many entrepreneurs initially seek to capture the returns to the develop-

Stop! Don't Do It!

1. Don't try to protect your new product or service against imitation through the use of a brand name when your product or service is first introduced.

2. Don't use a strategy to build a brand name unless advertising is effective as a way to convince customers that other products or services are not worthy substitutes.

ment of new products and services in other ways than through the development of brand names, and then shift to the use of reputation once the company has become larger and more established.

Learning Curves

Companies improve at making products as they produce more of them because experience at making and selling products provides information about how to do those things better. This concept, called the learning curve, means that firms gain advantages from experience. Firms that have more experience making and selling a product can often produce and sell that product more efficiently than competitors or can incorporate features that competitors cannot match. For example, Sony is able to produce compact disk players more cheaply than many new entrants to the business because it has figured out more efficient ways of manufacturing and selling those products than new entrants.

The learning curve provides a way for firms to capture the returns to introducing new products and services. By virtue of their experience producing a product, companies that have been offering a product for a long period of time can often produce that product more efficiently and with more features than can companies that are first offering a product.

The fact that the learning curve is a mechanism for capturing the returns to introducing a new product or service has two important implications for you as a technology entrepreneur. Exploiting the learning curve cannot be the only mechanism that you use to capture the returns from introducing a new product or service at the time that you establish your firm. Learning curve advantages, by definition, are things that depend on experience. Therefore, at the time that your venture first begins, you cannot have a learning curve advantage over other firms started at the same time, and will have a learning curve disadvantage with respect to firms that were started previously.

Learning curve advantages depend heavily on the degree to which learning is proprietary. Some of the benefits of experience seep out to other companies in an industry even when they are farther down the learning curve than other companies. This means that you might not be able to exploit a learning curve advantage even if you started your company before others in the industry. For instance, many early Internet clothing retail start-ups were unable to stay ahead of later entrants. The later start-ups learned from the failures of companies with more experience in this business about the problems of trying to get people to buy products online without being able to try them on. Because this learning was not proprietary, it did not provide the early start-ups with a learning curve advantage.

If the benefits of experience that seep out to others cannot provide the basis for learning curve based advantages, then what things make a learning curve more proprietary and less subject to seepage? Learning that is based on tacit knowledge is one thing. It is more difficult to obtain tacit knowledge without producing something than it is to obtain codified knowledge without producing something because codified knowledge is available from documents, but tacit knowledge can only be gained by doing.

This is one reason why learning curve advantages are often a major mechanism for capturing the returns to the introduction of new products in the aircraft industry.[4] Aerospace engineers have developed a great deal of tacit knowledge by producing aircraft, and this knowledge is only available to those companies that employ these engineers. The learning curve is stronger in aerospace than in biotechnology, where more learning is codified and can be obtained by reading the articles and patents of firms already operating in the industry. In the latter case, the learning curve is less proprietary and therefore is less effective as a mechanism for capturing the returns to innovation.

Stop! Don't Do It!

1. Don't try to protect your new product or service through a learning curve advantage unless your business is founded at the start of an industry.

2. Don't try to protect your new product or service through a learning curve advantage unless learning is proprietary in your industry.

First Mover Advantage

Closely related to the concept of the learning curve is the concept of the first mover advantage. While a learning curve advantage is a benefit that accrues to an early entrant through the effects of experience on the ability to produce or sell products more efficiently and effectively, first mover advantages represent the benefits that accrue to early entrants from simply being first in the market, even if there are no gains from experience. For example, if a new company introduces a piece of accounting software, it may have a "first mover" advantage because the cost to customers of switching to competitor products later may be too high to justify the effort, thereby allowing them to retain customers even after competitors copy their products and services.

"First mover" advantages are very important to you, as a technology entrepreneur, because they can provide a mechanism for capturing the returns to new product introduction that works immediately from firm founding forward in time. Therefore, unlike learning curves and reputation effects, first mover advantages are very useful mechanisms for independent entrepreneurs, rather than just to the managers of large, established companies.

Unfortunately, being a first mover is not always an advantage. Being the first mover turns out to be an advantage when products or services face network externalities. Network externalities are a condition under which more value is created when there are more users. Think of telephones here. The more people who use telephones, the more valuable they are because the more likely it becomes that you can reach a person by phone.[5]

A good example of an entrepreneurial business that exploited first mover advantages that come from network externalities is eBay. Electronic auction houses have more value if they have more participants because, with more participants, there are more products to sell and more buyers looking at those products. Therefore, by getting customers first, eBay created an advantage that makes it harder for other firms to compete with them to attract customers.

Being a first mover is also an advantage any time the costs of switching from one product to another is high. Take computer software as an example. Customers face high costs to switching between the Apple and DOS operating systems. Once a particular operating system has been chosen, companies are largely locked in because their purchases of software are dependent on the operating system that they have chosen. Replacing a particular operating system requires writing off the entire investment in all software purchased.

Many graphics software products based on the Apple operating system proved to have a first mover advantage because customers found it difficult to switch to software based on the Windows operating system. Switching costs were high for customers because switching meant changing their computer hardware. Therefore, by being first to market, the producers of Apple-based software had an advantage over later entrants because they were based on an operating system that was very costly for customers to change.

Even if actual switching costs are low, first mover advantages exist when psychological switching costs are high. In general, people perceive a cost to switching products because they are biased in favor of the status quo.[6] Because people are biased toward the status quo, first movers face a lower cost for things like advertising that help to build a brand name. The initial company to develop a product pays less in

Stop! Don't Do It!

1. Don't try to protect your new product or service with a first mover advantage if customer switching costs are low.
2. Don't be a late mover in a business with network externalities.

advertising expenditure per customer attracted than any follower companies. Moreover, customers generally demand a premium to switch to a new product or service. Thus, the producers of a follower product have to invest more in promoting it to get equal recognition to the producers of a first product.[7] And, more important, a follower product has to be more than marginally better in terms of quality and features than a first product to get customers to switch. Because the first product becomes the benchmark against which later products are compared, customers tend to be willing to switch only when the later product represents a significant improvement on the initial product. The first mover's product has the advantage of being the default choice.[8]

Complementary Assets

A final mechanism to capture the returns from the introduction of new products and services that entrepreneurs need to consider is *complementary assets*. As was mentioned earlier, complementary assets are assets, such as distribution outlets and manufacturing plants that are used along with a new product or service.[9]

Complementary assets allow companies to sell their products and services successfully even if they are less innovative than competitor products and services. Take automobile sales as an example. Hyundai may be more innovative than General Motors, but General Motors might still sell more of its vehicles in the United States than Hyundai.

Hyundai lacks dealerships (a complementary asset to the innovative car product) in many parts of the United States. As a result, General Motors can sell a less innovative product than Hyundai just because its complementary assets are better.

In general, complementary assets are not something that you, as a technology entrepreneur, can use to exploit your new product or service. You and other technology entrepreneurs like you are not going to have manufacturing and marketing complementary assets in place when you create your firms, while your established firm competitors probably have those assets in place. Therefore, established firms usually are the beneficiaries of the use of complementary assets to capture the returns from the introduction of new products and services.

Even though you are unlikely to benefit from the exploitation of complementary assets, the use of them to capture the returns to new product introduction is important to you because they explain why your new business stands a good chance of failing when you seek to compete with large established companies even if you have innovative products that customers like.

To understand why new companies with innovative products often lose out in competition with large established firms that control the complementary assets in marketing and distribution, you first have to understand the problem of imitation. As the previous chapter explained, innovative new products are often very easy to imitate. Patents provide a way to deter that imitation, but only in those situations when patents are effective. In industries, like biotechnology, where patents are effective and when patents offer broad scope claims that deter imitation, you and other technology entrepreneurs like you often can introduce new products and services successfully. When patent protection is strong, the patent creates a barrier to imitation by other firms.[10]

The situation is more complicated when patent protection is weak. This is the case in many industries, like consumer electronics, in which patents are very easy to get around. Here your ability to start a firm and profit from the introduction of new products or services depends a lot on whether the industry has a dominant design—a common way that all products or services are set up in an industry.[11]

If an industry has not yet converged on a dominant design, then it is hard to say whether your new firm will capture the returns to the introduction of a new product or service. Success before a dominant design is in place depends on what product designs are favored by different niche markets and what design ultimately becomes dominant. If you come up with a design that appeals to a valuable niche market, or a design that ultimately becomes the dominant design, then you can capture the returns to the introduction of new products or services.[12]

The story is very different if the industry has already converged on a dominant design, but patent protection is weak. Weak patent protection means that it is very easy for a large established company to imitate your (or any other entrepreneur's) new product or service. Because a dominant design is in place, the products and services that companies produce need to be very similar to one another. Under these conditions, success in an industry depends largely on who has better marketing or manufacturing. Better marketing and manufacturing allows a company to produce a version of a very similar product to those offered by competitors more cheaply.

This is where complementary assets become important. Firms that have existing manufacturing facilities and distribution outlets under their control are better able to benefit from the introduction of new products or services. Unlike new firms, which first have to gain control over manufacturing and distribution to introduce a new product or service, established firms can exploit their existing manufacturing and distribution assets to introduce the new product or service more cheaply or more effectively than new firms. Thus, as long as the established firms can imitate the products that new firms introduce, they have an advantage over the new firms at providing those products to customers.[13]

Industries in which patent protection is weak and the firms in it have converged on a dominant product design are not very favorable to new firms. However, it is still possible for you to succeed in these industries. To be successful, you need to gain control of complementary assets as quickly as possible. How do you do that? By contracting for them. Building them from scratch usually takes too long.[14]

If the complementary assets are not specialized, this strategy can work. For instance, if the marketing and distribution outlets are generic—any retail store will do—then you can often get a contract with someone to distribute the new product or service. Then, unless the established company has much better marketing and distribution outlets than the ones that you contracted for, you have a chance to compete.

However, if the complementary assets are specialized, then this strategy is very unlikely to be successful. Specialized complementary assets are assets that are used along with the new product or service, but are not generic. A good example of a specialized complementary asset is a piece of manufacturing equipment that can only be used to produce a particular product.

The problem with contracting for specialized assets as a strategy to obtain control over them is that it is hard to sign a contract to have someone manufacture or distribute a product for you if they have to make a specialized investment to do it. Why? Once they make that specialized investment, they are dependent on your company—after all they just made a specialized investment in what you do—and this dependency makes them vulnerable to your opportunistic actions. You would be in a very good position to strike a better deal by exploiting their dependence. As a result, most of the time that complementary assets are specialized, firms find it difficult to gain control of them through contracting, and have to own them.[15]

Stop! Don't Do It!

1. Don't try to start a firm in an industry with weak patent protection and a dominant design. You will probably fail.
2. Don't try to contract for specialized complementary assets. You will have a hard time finding a partner.

This need for ownership is what dooms you in your effort to establish a new firm. New companies can rarely obtain enough capital to put in place an efficient marketing or manufacturing system, at founding, and even if they can, they generally cannot work out the kinks in operating those new systems quickly enough to compete with established firms.

A good example of this situation is the automobile industry. Manufacturing and distribution in the automobile industry are controlled by the major automakers. Patent protection is relatively weak

Questions to Ask Yourself

1. What will my new business's competitive advantage be?
2. Will obtaining control over resources help me capture the returns from introducing my new product or service?
3. Will establishing a reputation help me to capture the returns from introducing my new product or service?
4. Will I be able to capture the returns from introducing my new product or service by being a first mover?
5. Will I be able to capture the returns from introducing my new product or service by moving up the learning curve ahead of competitors?
6. Will I be able to gain control over complementary assets or will I fail to capture the returns from introducing my new product or service because large established firms control the complementary assets that I need?

because most automobile components are mechanical or electrical devices. A dominant design exists in the internal combustion design. Moreover, the production of automobiles involves specialized manufacturing equipment. As a result, we almost never see successful new companies founded to introduce new products or services in the automobile industry.

Summary

In addition to the use of patents and secrecy described in the previous chapter, firms capture the returns from the introduction of new products and services through the control of resources, building brand-name reputations, exploiting learning curves, first mover advantages, and control of complementary assets in manufacturing and marketing. This chapter explained how each of these appropriability mechanisms affects you as a technology entrepreneur seeking to set up a successful new company.

Controlling resources is a strategy in which you buy up or contracts for the key sources of supply for producing the new product or service. This strategy is most effective when there is a bottleneck in the production process, making one resource crucial and rare.

Establishing a reputation is a strategy in which you invest in advertising to create a brand name. The brand name deters customers from shifting to competing products by creating the perception that the entrepreneur's product has features that make it worth additional cost. However, because advertising takes time to work and is subject to economies of scale, this method of capturing the returns to the introduction of new products and services does not work well for most technology entrepreneurs.

Exploiting the learning curve is a strategy in which one firm moves ahead of other firms in terms of efficiency as a result of learning from the process of delivering a product or service. Exploiting a learning curve is most effective as a strategy when an entrepreneur is an early entrant in an industry and when the knowledge gained from experience is proprietary. However, exploiting the learning curve is not likely to be an effective strategy for capturing the returns to new product or service introduction when you first found your firm.

Being the first mover is a strategy in which you benefit from being the first provider of a product or service, even when there is nothing to be gained from experience. Being a first mover can be an advantage or a disadvantage. It is an advantage when network externalities exist and when real or psychological switching costs are high. The first mover advantage can be effective in capturing the returns to new product or service introduction when you first found your firm.

A final strategy involves exploiting complementary assets—other assets that are used jointly to deliver a new product or service—as the basis of the firm's competitive advantage. This strategy is most effective when patent protection in an industry is weak, and the industry has converged on a dominant design. In general, as a technology entrepreneur, you will have a hard time competing in industries in which complementary assets are important because you are unlikely to have these assets in place at the time that your company is founded. If these assets are not specialized, then you can contract for these assets and sometimes compete with established firms. However, when complementary assets are specialized, you stand virtually no chance of success because then you cannot obtain control over those assets through contracting, leaving you without a way to obtain these assets before established firms imitate your new product or service.

Now that you understand rule number eight of technology entrepreneurship, appropriate the returns to innovation, we now turn to rule number nine, choose the right organizational form, which is the subject of the next chapter.

9

CHOOSING
THE RIGHT
ORGANIZATIONAL
FORM

Most people believe that entrepreneurship involves creating a new firm that does all of its own product development, production, and distribution. Although it is true that entrepreneurs often use hierarchical approaches to exploiting opportunities, by creating new organizations that own all stages of the value chain from purchasing supplies to marketing and distribution, you can also exploit opportunities with more market-based mechanisms, such as licensing or strategic alliances. For example, biotechnology start-ups often partner with large pharmaceutical firms either through licensing or strategic alliances in which the actual drug production, and even development and FDA approval, is undertaken by the pharmaceutical firms. Therefore, an important question for you to consider as you plan to become a technology entrepreneur is, What is the right mode of exploitation for my opportunity?

In general, several different sets of factors affect this decision: Cost, speed, capabilities, and information.[1] The sections of this chapter each examine one of these four sets of factors. We begin with the cost of exploitation.

Cost of Exploitation

What if you discovered an opportunity to introduce a new tissue grasper for use in surgery, but lacked the several million dollars that it takes to get FDA approval for a new surgical device? While you might tap a business angel or venture capitalist for the money that you need, you might decide to license the invention to an established medical device firm instead.

You can use licensing and other market-based modes of opportunity exploitation when the cost of exploiting an opportunity is high and you lack adequate capital to exploit the opportunity through other means. In fact, technology entrepreneurs who have less capital or less ability to raise money in capital markets tend to use market-based modes of opportunity exploitation more than other technology entrepreneurs.

Moreover, market-based modes of opportunity exploitation are particularly important when the technology opportunities that you are planning to exploit are capital intensive. The lack of cash flow from existing activities means that you must obtain capital from financial markets. Because you will know much more about your business idea than any potential investors, you will need to pay investors a risk premium to compensate them for the asymmetry of information between you and them. This risk premium means that externally raised capital is more expensive than internally raised capital. This excess cost of capital becomes more problematic for you as your need for capital rises. As a result, you should be more likely to use market-oriented modes of opportunity exploitation as the capital intensity of a production process rises.[2]

Stop! Don't Do It!

1. Don't try to own the whole value chain if your opportunity is expensive to exploit.
2. Don't try to own the whole value chain if you lack capital.

Accelerating the Pace to Market

Another reason to use market-oriented modes of opportunity exploitation is to speed the time to market. Very often entrepreneurial opportunities are short-lived because they depend on an external change that will quickly close up. Take, for example, the source of an opportunity for a new electronic voting machine that resulted from the problems with hanging chads in the 2000 presidential election. The nature of this problem and the frequency of elections mean that anyone wishing to sell new electronic voting machines had to get a new product developed and sold within a relatively short period. Because of the time that it takes to create a value chain, establishing the entire voting machine value chain from scratch might lead you to miss the window of opportunity if you started a company to exploit this opportunity. To avoid this problem, you could establish the value chain through contractual means. Because contracting allows the value chain to be assembled more quickly than creating the value chain assets through a hierarchical mode of operation, it allows you to meet the window of opportunity.

You can also use contractual modes of opportunity exploitation when there are reasons to enter a market quickly even if the opportunity is long-lived. For instance, entrepreneurs often use contractual models of opportunity exploitation when there are first mover advantages in an industry. By using contractual modes of exploitation, such as licensing and strategic alliances, you can get to market before competitors in industries with network externalities and high switching

Stop! Don't Do It!

1. Don't try to own the whole value chain when your business opportunity is short-lived.

2. Don't try to own the whole value chain when there are first mover advantages in your industry.

costs. As was explained earlier, quick entry to the market is often very beneficial in these types of industries.

Making Use of the Best Capabilities

Yet another reason to use contractual modes of opportunity exploitation is that you may not have the best capabilities to exploit the opportunity. For instance, established firms often have better marketing and manufacturing capabilities or knowledge of the customer than you do. (This of course was the point about the benefits of complementary assets in the exploitation of opportunities made in the last chapter.) If this is the case, you may be able reap greater profits from licensing the opportunity to an established firm. Not only does licensing the opportunity reduce the cost of exploitation because the established firm is going to be more efficient and effective at exploiting it than you are, but also this arrangement reduces the need to create duplicative assets.[3] The established company probably doesn't have to establish new retail outlets or a new manufacturing plant to take advantage of the opportunity, but you would have to duplicate the established company's investment in these assets if you exploited the opportunity directly. Therefore, licensing is very good idea if you realize that your capabilities at exploitation are inferior to those of existing firms.

A good example of this situation is the licensing of technologies by university inventors. Anyone who has spent even a few moments in a science or engineering department of a major research university will soon realize that most faculty do not know much about how to create new technology companies. As a rule, they almost always know less than the managers of established companies about such things as persuading customers to buy products, managing employees, and creating manufacturing plants. As a result, most university inventors are better off licensing their inventions to established companies rather than starting their own firms.

There is one important trade-off here. In many cases, the knowledge of how to develop a new product or service is tacit and held in the minds of the inventor. As a result, it is very hard to develop a new product or service without the inventor's involvement. Under these circumstances, inventors often become entrepreneurs even through they have worse capabilities than established firm managers. Without inventor involvement, the invention simply cannot be turned into a new product or service, and the necessity of involving inventors trumps the importance of strong capabilities at business development.

Nature of the Technology

Some types of technologies can be exploited more effectively through hierarchical modes of exploitation—that is, a single company owning product development, manufacturing and distribution—whereas oth-

Stop! Don't Do It!

1. Don't try to exploit your opportunity on your own if you have worse capabilities than existing firms.

2. Don't license the opportunity when the key skills to exploit the new product or service are tacit and so reside only in your own head.

ers can be exploited more effectively through contractual modes (things like licensing or strategic alliances). In particular, researchers have identified crucial dimensions of technologies that make them more appropriate for one mode versus another. Contractual modes of exploitation are more effective when technologies are discrete (things that can be used alone, such as a drug), while hierarchical modes are more effective when technologies are systemic (things that can only be used in conjunction with other things, such as computer software). Because systemic technologies require coordination across the different components, hierarchical modes of opportunity exploitation, which help to ensure that the entities producing the components are coordinated, are useful. For example, if you plan to develop a video game that has both hardware and software components, you probably want to use a hierarchical approach in which your company owns both the production of the hardware and the software. If you only owned the hardware portion and contracted with someone else to produce the software, you might have trouble ensuring that the software fit the hardware correctly.[4]

Where technologies are based on codified knowledge, as opposed to tacit knowledge, market-based modes of exploitation are more effective. Why? Because contracts can be written more easily and effectively when knowledge is more codified than when it is tacit. To coordinate independent organizations in the process of developing a technology, the ability to write enforceable contracts is an important precondition. If information cannot be codified, contracts become problematic because it will be hard for either party to enforce any agreement that they have made, if they can even come to agreement in the first place.[5]

Take, for example, an idea for a new business to produce a new composite material. If you cannot codify how you will make the material, you are going to have a hard time licensing this new technology to others. Anyone who buys the technology is going to want to know how to produce the material, and will lack the tacit knowledge that you may have for doing so. Moreover, if you cannot codify the process, it may be very difficult to specify the cost of the process. Without specifying the cost, most buyers are going to be quite reluctant to commit to a contract in the first place.

Where technical standards exist, market-based mechanisms of opportunity exploitation are more viable than where no technical standards exist because technical standards facilitate the coordination of activity between independent firms.[6] Why? Because independent companies can be confident that anyone that they need to coordinate with is adhering to standards that make their products compatible. Therefore, you can start a company to produce application software today without having to own the company that produces the system software that will run the application. Technical standards now exist for system software that allow you to contract with the providers of that software without running the risk of incompatibility.

Where complementary assets are specialized, hierarchical modes of opportunity exploitation are more effective. One of the major dimensions of a business that firms have to decide whether to vertically integrate is manufacturing and marketing complementary assets. If complementary assets are not specialized to the purpose to which they will be used, then it is cheaper and less risky to contract for them. For instance, it is often cheaper to contract with a delivery firm to deliver your product than it is to buy trucks for the same purpose. However, if complementary assets are specialized, say manufacturing equipment that has to be customized to make your product,

Stop! Don't Do It!

1. Don't use contracting when the technology on which your new product or service is based is systemic.

2. Don't use contracting when there is no technical standard for your new product or service.

you will need to own them. As you no doubt remember from the previous chapter, people will not make irreversible commitments for specialized assets because they will be afraid of being taken advantage of by opportunistic partners.[7]

Managing Information Problems in Organizing

You will also need to consider information problems when you choose between owning the different parts of the value chain and contracting for them. Depending on the nature of the business, the information problems from contractual modes sometimes outweigh the information problems from hierarchical modes. When this is the case, you are best off adopting hierarchical modes and adopting contractual modes when the opposite is true.

One type of information problem that makes it important to own the different parts of the value chain is the disclosure problem. As chapter 7 explained, you need to keep information about your opportunity secret to prevent other people from imitating your new product or service. One of the problems with using contracts to obtain control over manufacturing or distribution outlets is that to set up a contract with someone else to provide these things, you will to disclose your secrets to them. This need to divulge information often creates what Nobel Prize–winning economist Kenneth Arrow called the *disclosure paradox*. If you want to license the technology to an existing manufacturer and have that company manufacture your product for you, you need to tell the manufacturer what the new technology will do. After all, the manufacturer will not want to contract to pay you for the new technology without evidence that it has value. Unfortunately, your efforts to provide the manufacturer with evidence that your new technology has value will demonstrate to the buyer how the technology works, which lets the manufacturer know what you know. Once the manufacturer knows what you know, he or she has no reason to pay you to license your knowledge—you just gave it away for free! Hence, there is a paradox of disclosure.[8]

While disclosure problems can be mitigated in a number of ways, the best way to mitigate them is through patenting. Because patents preclude a potential buyer of your knowledge from making a duplicative product or service without a license from you, they allow you to disclose your invention to a potential buyer without the risk of having its value appropriated without compensation by the potential buyer. Of course, the reduction in this risk facilitates the use of market-oriented modes of opportunity exploitation, such as licensing.

Other information problems enhance your ability to use contractual rather than hierarchical modes of opportunity exploitation. For instance, suppose that you have developed a new technology for making eyeglasses. You might choose to use a contractual mode of opportunity exploitation, such as franchising, to mitigate adverse selection and moral hazard problems. The potential for adverse selection—potential employees misrepresenting their abilities to gain a job, for instance—makes franchising a good approach to exploiting a business.

The managers of eyeglass stores are typically paid largely through straight wages. For this reason, a person who gets hired for a job as an eyeglass store manager has an incentive to tell a potential employer that he or she is a better store manager than he or she really is, so as to get the job. If the person turns out to be only an average store manager and so generates only half as much store revenue as an above average manager, that person will not bear any of the cost of this outcome. The person will get paid the same wage as they would have been paid if they turned out to be an above average manager. All of the difference in the performance of the eyeglass store that results from the difference between having a below average and an above average manager is borne by the store's owner.

This problem is mitigated by franchising. Because a franchisee has to invest in purchasing the outlet that he or she will run, and then

receives compensation from his or her profits from running the outlet, that person does not have an incentive to misrepresent his or her
abilities. Because people with only average skills and capabilities will
earn only average profits from operating a franchised eyeglass store,
they will be less inclined to purchase an eyeglass franchise than people with above average skills and capabilities, who will earn above
average profits from operating that store.[9] Therefore, the use of franchising allows you to overcome the adverse selection problem and
find better outlet operators than would be the case without franchising.

When you set up your company, you also face the problem of the
shirking of effort by your employees. When people cannot earn any
additional compensation by working harder, they often shirk and do
not work as hard as they possibly can. This is often the case when people are paid a straight salary that is not directly linked to how hard
they work or the effect of their efforts on profits. Contractual modes
of opportunity exploitation, like franchising, mitigate the shirking
problem because they provide an incentive for your employees to
work harder. By replacing an employee's wage with a share of profits,
franchising links the compensation that you pay employees to their
effort, which provides employees with an incentive to work harder.
Thus, you can use contractual modes of opportunity exploitation to
reduce the shirking problem.[10]

On the other hand, contractual modes of opportunity exploitation
increase a problem called free riding. Free riding is the tendency of
one party to let all other parties do the work necessary to receive a
benefit. A good example of free riding is the tendency for the owners
of a chain of eyeglass stores that operate under the same brand name
to each let the others conduct the advertising to promote the chain to
customers.

When there is only one store in an advertising market, the owner
of that store will want to advertise the chain. Why? Because the ben-

efits of advertising that come in the form of additional sales will be captured by the store owner. However, if the eyeglass store is a chain that is owned by several different people, the situation is not so simple. Under the latter scenario, each dollar of advertising will still attract the same number of customers, but now each store owner has the opportunity to get customers without paying for the advertising. If the owners of all of the other outlets of the chain pay for the advertising, then the remaining owner can benefit by free riding off of their efforts.

Because customers will go to the outlet that is most convenient for them regardless of who paid for the advertising, the outlet owner who did not pay for the ad will still get his or her share of customers. However, now he or she will get these customers without paying for the advertising, which is a more profitable way to get customers. The incentive for each of the outlet operators to free ride is mitigated if all of the outlets are owned by the same company, and the outlets are managed by employees. Because employees will not benefit from free riding, they have no incentive to engage in it. (Why do something that is not socially acceptable if you get no benefit from doing it?) Therefore, the employees who manage the stores will not try to get out of paying for the advertising, making noncontractual modes of opportunity exploitation more effective than contractual modes of opportunity exploitation in this situation.

Another problem that reduces the likelihood that a company will use a contractual form of opportunity exploitation is called "holdup." This is a situation in which one party takes advantage of another's vulnerabilities to renegotiate an agreement to its benefit. An example of holdup occurs when a company licensing a technology requires the licensee to invest in very specific manufacturing equipment that can only be used to produce the licensor's product. Then the licensor demands that the licensee pay better terms on the agreement, say a higher royalty rate. Because the licensee's alternative is to write off

Stop! Don't Do It!

1. Don't disclose the value of your new product or service to a potential partner, unless it is protected by a patent.

2. Don't use contracting when the problems of holdup and freeriding are greater than the problems of adverse selection and shirking in your business.

his or her investment in the specific equipment or pay the higher royalty rate, he or she will accept the new, worse, terms. After all, accepting new terms is still better than writing off the investment.[11] Because potential licensees are afraid of the possibility of holdup, they are often reluctant to work with potential licensors. As a result, if you are going to ask your licensees to invest in specialized equipment, you are going to find it hard to attract licensing partners. Under these circumstances, you are better off engaging in more hierarchical modes of opportunity exploitation.

Questions to Ask Yourself

1. Is my opportunity too expensive for me to exploit by owning the entire value chain?

2. Do I have time to develop the value chain on my own or do I need to get to market too quickly to create the value chain from scratch?

3. Do I have the capabilities to exploit the opportunity on my own?

4. Is my technology a type that can be exploited easily through contracting?

5. Are the information problems created by contracting greater or less than the information problems created by owning the entire value chain?

Summary

This chapter explained that you do not always have to create a new company that owns all stages of the value chain from product development to manufacturing to distribution as a way to exploit an opportunity. You can also use contractual modes such as licensing and strategic alliances. Contractual modes of opportunity exploitation are good to use when opportunities are expensive to exploit. They are also good to use when you need to exploit opportunities quickly, and do not have time to build the value chain from scratch. It is a good idea to use contractual modes when you lack the capabilities to exploit the opportunities yourself. You should use hierarchical modes of opportunity exploitation when the technologies that they are exploiting are systemic, based on tacit knowledge, face no technical standards, and where complementary assets are specialized. Finally, you should use hierarchical modes of opportunity exploitation when the information problems of disclosure, holdup, and free riding are dominant; and use contractual modes of exploitation when the information problems of employee adverse selection and shirking are dominant.

Now that you understand rule number nine of technology entrepreneurship, select the right organizational form, we now turn to rule number ten, manage risk and uncertainty, which is the subject of the next chapter.

10

MANAGING RISK AND UNCERTAINTY

As the previous chapters have discussed, when you found a new technology company you are going to face a variety of sources of uncertainty that need to be managed. For instance, when you start your company, the market may not yet exist for the product or service that you are introducing, leading the company to face market uncertainty. Similarly, you may not be sure how to create that product or service, generating technological uncertainty. Moreover, even if you can create the product or service and there is a market for it, you will face competitive uncertainty because you cannot know for sure whether you can capture the returns from introducing the product or service or if those returns will flow to competitors.

This chapter:

- Explains how successful entrepreneurs manage uncertainty in the process of developing new technology companies

- Describes the problems that uncertainty imposes on new technology companies

- Explains why you must either reduce uncertainty or give share-holders a greater portion of returns as a way to manage the start-up problem

- Discusses the risk reduction strategies that you should employ

- Talks about the approaches you can use to reallocate risk to those better able to bear it

- Discusses the strategies that you can use to manage percep-tions of risk

- Identifies two tools that you can use to manage risk: real options and scenario analysis

- Explains how you can convince stakeholders to bear risk for you

The Start-up Problem

The process of developing a new technology company involves the management of significant uncertainty. As you might expect, this uncertainty impacts the financing of new ventures. To exploit a technology opportunity, you will generally have to obtain resources from outside sources. Therefore, you have to convince external stakeholders to provide support resources, despite the uncertainty that the new venture faces.

The more uncertainty that your new venture faces, the greater the return that investors and other stakeholders will demand to provide the resources that you need to exploit your opportunity. The relationship between uncertainty and desired returns means that you are faced with the following options: You can provide stakeholders with greater equity in the new venture as a way to increase the size of the returns that investors will earn for a given amount of invested capital. You can bear the uncertainty yourself, or you can adopt strategies to manage uncertainty.

Successful technology entrepreneurs tend to prefer the latter alternative. The first alternative is not desirable to many entrepreneurs because they do not want to give up ownership and control of their new ventures. Moreover, many investors do not like the idea of assuming majority ownership and control of new ventures that they finance because such an arrangement leads to incentive problems. The second alternative is not desirable to many entrepreneurs because people are risk averse and do not usually like to bear uncertainty.

Risk Reduction Strategies

Successful technology entrepreneurs often manage risk and uncertainty by engaging in three activities to reduce the risk that their new ventures face: searching for information, minimizing investment, and maintaining flexibility. You will need to engage in these risk reduction strategies to be successful.

Searching for Information

You need to search for information before taking action if you want to reduce the level of risk in your new venture. Unsuccessful technology entrepreneurs often fire before they take aim. As a result, they bear unnecessary risks that could be easily avoided by searching for additional information. For instance, instead of figuring out what type of manufacturing equipment is most appropriate for producing a new product, the typical unsuccessful entrepreneur goes out and gets the standard equipment used in the industry and "gets started." If, as is sometimes the case, the equipment chosen needs to be modified heavily to make the product, the entrepreneur has now set him or herself up to bear the risk that the modification cannot be done correctly or in time to meet a market window.

This is an example where risk could be reduced by searching for information before acting. If the entrepreneur had spent more time figuring out what type of equipment was most appropriate for his or her new business, then the risk of failing to modify the equipment could have been avoided.

Given that searching for information is an effective way to minimize the risk that you bear in starting your new venture, understanding how to search for information that reduces risk is important. Therefore, you should plan rather than just act. You should think about and evaluate opportunities before acting on them, and you do not take action until you have a reason to take action. By planning, you can avoid taking action that is unnecessary and avoid chasing down low-probability outcomes.

In the context of new ventures, planning often involves the formulation of a business plan and financial statements. These documents present your approach to developing the business, its risks, its use of funds, and the interrelationships of different parts of the venture. Research has shown that entrepreneurs who develop business plans are more likely to survive, develop their businesses faster, and have higher sales than entrepreneurs that do not develop business plans.[1] Developing a business plan is one of the ways that you can search for information, thereby reducing the uncertainty that your new venture must bear.

Successful entrepreneurs also minimize risk by proving the accuracy of their assumptions before committing resources. Many entrepreneurial efforts are uncertain because they are based on assumptions about such things as technical feasibility or market size on which information that proves or disproves these assumptions is available. For example, entrepreneurs often make assumptions about things like whether one can make a microchip small enough to fit in a watch or the size of the market for a drug to treat pancreatic cancer. These assumptions can be tested through the search for information. Before taking action you could ask a semiconductor engineer if it is possible to make a microchip that fits in a watch or ask an oncologist how many patients could be cured with a drug for pancreatic cancer. If a source can provide information that determines the accuracy of your assumptions, you can minimize the uncertainty of your new business by seeking out that information prior to starting the business.

Successful entrepreneurs search for information by exploring the relationships between the dimensions of their business. One source of uncertainty for new businesses lies in information about how the parts of a business are related. For example, a lack of knowledge about the relationship between each dollar of cost and each dollar of sales makes the new venture uncertain; the effect of incurring particular costs on outcomes is not clear. This uncertainty can be mitigated by gathering information about the relationship between different parts of the business.

Successful entrepreneurs seek disconfirming information. That is, they look for information that will show why their new ventures will not work, rather than information that shows why the venture will work. Why? Most people engage in decision-making biases that lead them to seek confirming information that supports decisions that they have already committed to making. As a result, most people do not gather information that is useful to evaluation, but instead engage in justification of their own actions. Successful entrepreneurs refrain from justifying their own actions by seeking disconfirming information.

This problem is further exacerbated by the tendency of entrepreneurs to be overoptimistic about the prospects for their ventures. This overoptimism leads entrepreneurs to move forward with their ventures even when a rational evaluation of the opportunity would show that the likelihood of success is lower than the entrepreneur believes it to be. This overoptimism also leads most entrepreneurs to discount information that might lead them to realistically conclude that entrepreneurial activity does not make sense. Successful entrepreneurs keep their optimism in check by seeking disconfirming information about the value of their new ventures.

Minimizing Investment

You will need to minimize the magnitude of your investments in non-salvageable assets if you want to reduce the level of risk in your new venture. Successful entrepreneurs minimize their investments in assets with low salvage value because risk is very much affected by the magnitude of what a person will lose if things turn out badly. With investments in assets with high salvage value, even if the venture is unsuccessful, the value of the investment will be recouped. Thus, you can make larger investments for a given amount of risk if you invest in assets that have more salvage value than if you invest in assets that have less salvage value.

What practical steps can you follow to minimize your investment in assets with low salvage value? One step is to use standard inputs rather than customized ones. For instance, you can use generic office equipment instead of customized office equipment. In the event that your business fails, you can sell the generic office equipment to another business, increasing the salvage value of the asset. However, the investment in the customized office equipment is lost because it cannot be used in any other business.[2]

Of course, sometimes you will need to use customized inputs. After all, generic inputs cannot provide the basis of a competitive advantage. This suggests the importance of considering whether assets are the source of your business's competitive advantage. Many inputs into new businesses do not provide a competitive advantage and should not be customized. For example, back office accounting software is unlikely to be the source of competitive advantage for a medical device firm. Investment in this customized input increases risk for the new venture without offering a compensating competitive advantage. As a result, it has no value and should be avoided.

Another step is to borrow or lease assets rather than purchasing them. For instance, you can lease the trucks for your new business needs instead of buying them. By borrowing or leasing assets, you can minimize the investment that you have to make in assets that have limited salvage value in the event of failure.

Yet another step is to make investments in the form of variable costs rather than fixed costs. Variable costs are costs that are dependent on the production of a good or service. Variable costs impose less risk on new ventures than fixed costs because with fixed costs, there are up-front expenditures that may or may not ever be made up, imposing risk on whoever paid for those up-front expenditures.

How can you keep your fixed costs low when you start your business? One way is to start your new firm as consulting organization first and expand into manufacturing products only if there is sufficient demand to do so.[3] For example, you might first develop a service for providing accounting software to other companies. Then, if the software proves popular, you can transition to producing the software as a shrink-wrapped product, rather than as a service.

Another way for you to keep fixed costs low is to look for mechanisms that transform fixed costs into variable costs. For example, using a contract manufacturer or a contract sales force in place of building a manufacturing plant or hiring employees is a way of turning the fixed cost of manufacturing or sales and distribution into variable cost because the contract manufacturer or sales force is paid on a per unit basis.

Of course, no matter how hard you try you are going to have to invest in some fixed assets that have zero salvage value. To minimize the risk of this type of investment, successful entrepreneurs often begin on a small scale and expand from there. That is, instead of establishing factories on a large scale with broad product lines, you can start on a small scale with a single product. Only if you are successful with that initial effort, do you expand. This approach minimizes risk because you can only lose the amount of capital that has been invested in the venture. Because the total amount of capital invested in a new venture is smaller if the venture begins on a small scale, you can minimize risk by starting this way.[4]

Another step to minimizing investment in new ventures is to decide in advance the point at which you will cut your losses and move on. Unfortunately, many unsuccessful entrepreneurs start businesses like gamblers with open credit lines in Las Vegas. They increase their investments over time, thinking that one more dollar of investment will turn the corner for their new ventures. However, this type of thinking leads unsuccessful entrepreneurs to increase the magnitude of their losses through escalation of commitment.

Maintaining Flexibility

You can also minimize the risk of starting a new business by maintaining flexibility so that your new company can change direction rapidly if that becomes necessary. Flexibility reduces risk because it minimizes the probability that a downside loss will occur. While you can't know in advance of starting a new venture if you can overcome technical, market, and competitive uncertainty, you can still avoid a downside loss if you change your venture when unexpected events occur. If your new venture can shift under these circumstances, then your probability of being stuck in a situation in which the downside loss occurs will be reduced.

Take, for example, the story of the successful developers of the latest generation of computer disk drives. These companies managed the risk of introducing a new product with an uncertain market by

Stop! Don't Do It!

1. Don't act before you investigate when starting your new business.
2. Don't make large investments in assets with low salvage value.
3. Don't take actions that reduce the flexibility of your new venture.

being flexible and adaptive. The disk drive start-ups initially targeted a set of customers that turned out not to want the new disk drives that they were offering. As a result, the start-ups had to shift target markets until they found one interested in adopting the new product.[5] The ability to be adaptive and find a market segment interested in their new products allowed the entrepreneurs behind these ventures to manage market risk in the introduction of a new disk drive product.

Risk Reallocation Strategies

You can also manage risk and uncertainty by reallocating risks to other parties. In many cases, these other parties are willing to accept this reallocated risk because they are better able to bear that risk than you are. For instance, diversified investors are often better able to bear risk than entrepreneurs because of their diversification. Investors, like venture capital firms, that are able to invest simultaneously in several risky ventures can bear risk better than entrepreneurs whose investments in new ventures are undiversified. By simultaneously investing in several new ventures, venture capitalists can design portfolios in which the risks of different ventures are uncorrelated, making the average level of risk that they bear lower than that of the individual entrepreneurs that founded the companies in their portfolios. As a result, diversified investors can bear a level of risk for given amount of return that is not possible for individual entrepreneurs to bear.

You can reallocate risk to specialized stakeholders who are better able to bear risk than you and other entrepreneurs because their specialization gives them information that makes the risk less for them than for you. For example, a factor (or company that purchases accounts receivable) can collect your bills with less risk than you can because the factor has knowledge about collection of debt that allows for the collection of a greater proportion of receivables than the average entrepreneur. As a result, specialized stakeholders are willing to bear more risk for a given amount of return than you are probably willing to bear.[6]

You can reallocate risk to stakeholders who are engaged in existing activity at less than full capacity because their other activities make the risk of engaging in the new activity lower for them than for you. Take, for example, someone with a plant that is operating at half capacity. They can produce your product by just using the part of their plant that is idle, but you would have to create a new plant from scratch to produce the same product. As a result, they have a lower downside loss than you do for undertaking the same activity, making the activity less risky for them than for you.[7]

You can reallocate risk to stakeholders who are risk seeking. Business angels are a good example of people that are willing to bear your risk for you even though they are not better able to bear that risk than you are. Because business angels enjoy the entrepreneurial process, they are often willing to bear risk in return for allowing them to participate in the entrepreneurial process.

Risk Perception Strategies

Another way that you can manage risk in new ventures is by seeking to reduce your stakeholders' perceptions of risk. While risk perception strategies do not reduce actual risk or reallocate those risks to

Stop! Don't Do It!

1. Don't bear risk if you can reallocate it to someone more capable of bearing it than you.
2. Don't bear risk when risk seekers are willing to bear it for you.

others, but merely reduce the sense that others have of the risk associated with a new venture, they are nevertheless important to successful risk management by entrepreneurs.

You can reduce the perception of risk in new ventures by seeking endorsement of your venture by high-status actors. For example, you might enter into a strategic alliance or other type of partnership with an established firm, much as new biotechnology companies do with large pharmaceutical firms. This alliance will allow you to use the support of the established company to bolster the perception that your venture is valuable even when that value is uncertain. Because the established firm risks its reputation if your new venture proves not to have value, the endorsement by the established firm is a credible signal of your new venture's value.[8]

Similarly, you can obtain the endorsement of government officials, the press, or other people in authority as ways to create positive perceptions of the value of your venture. People tend to perceive as less risky and more valuable those things that people in authority support. For instance, research has shown when companies win certification contests by magazines—such as the *Good Housekeeping* Seal of Approval—they are perceived by potential stakeholders as more valuable and less risky than other companies.[9]

Another way for you to mitigate the perception of risk about your new venture is to make sure that your new venture conforms to the rules, norms, routines, and procedures of the status quo. For instance, many new companies that exploit the new Ethernet technologies take great pains to explain to customers that their products are consistent with older Ethernet technologies. This, of course, makes customers more comfortable transitioning to the new technology. What makes this approach interesting is that the new Ethernet technologies actually have very little to do with the old Ethernet technologies—the relationship between the two lies largely in their names.

By making your new venture look as much like established businesses as possible, you can also minimize the perception by others

Stop! Don't Do It!

1. Don't flout rules, norms, routines, and procedures. It raises perceptions of the risk of your venture.
2. Don't ignore collective action. It can often mitigate perceptions of the risk of your venture.

that your business is risky. For instance, successful entrepreneurs who found businesses in their garages often use borrowed offices for their meetings to make their businesses look more typical and less risky than the start-ups that they really are.[10] By doing this, successful entrepreneurs can get large established firms to provide support that those companies would be less likely to provide if the new ventures did not adhere to the rules and norms of big business.

Still another way for you to mitigate the perception that your new venture is risky is to engage in collective action, through trade associations or standard setting bodies. Because these entities decide what activities in an industry are considered to be appropriate and normal, a new firm that is a participant in these organizations will appear more legitimate and less risky than other new firms.[11]

Tools for Managing Risk and Uncertainty

Successful entrepreneurs also use two financial tools for managing uncertainty: real options and scenario analysis. Real options are the right, but not the obligation, to make a future investment. Scenario analysis is the representation of investments under different assumptions about key factors that influence those investments. You should use these tools to manage uncertainty in your business because their use will help you to make better decisions about your new venture than if you do not use them.

These tools overcome many of the disadvantages of more standard estimates of discounted cash flow based on net present value calculations. Standard net present value calculations do not accommodate uncertainty. Because they rely on point estimates, net present value calculation, do not deal well with a range of probabilities. Thus, any effort to use net present value calculations requires the user to simplify uncertainty by replacing uncertain things with point estimates. As a result, real options and scenario analysis help entrepreneurs to make more accurate decisions under uncertainty.

The accuracy of net present value calculations also depends very much on the accuracy of assumptions that are hard to verify at the time the calculations are typically made. For example, these calculations require accurate assumptions about the terminal value of an investment, which is very hard to know if things are truly uncertain. After all, if you do not know whether the product you are considering can be produced, whether there is a market for it, and whether you can withstand competition from other firms, it is hard to see how you can estimate the terminal value of an investment in a business to produce that product.

Similarly, these calculations require assumptions about the time horizons necessary to develop a product or service. Often such assumptions are very inaccurate before an entrepreneur begins to create a new product or service. Most of the time people simply do not know how long it will take them to create a new business or launch a new product. The requirement that assumptions about time horizons be made anyway are particularly problematic because estimates of time horizons that are too short will inflate net present value calculations and lead people to believe that an investment is better than it actually is. In contrast, estimates of time horizons that are too long will understate net present value calculations and lead people to believe that an investment is worse than it actually is.

Net present value calculations are also problematic for the evaluation of new venture opportunities because they cannot incorporate many important factors that influence decision making about those opportunities. For instance, they cannot incorporate nonfinancial information, such as reaction of competitors. Similarly, they cannot incorporate information about the strategic relationship of one part of the business to another, or learning in the process of innovation, both of which are often central to evaluating new venture opportunities.

Discounted cash flow based on net present value cannot evaluate things at successive stages. This is problematic for new technology ventures in which information is often not available for later stages until a venture has passed through earlier stages. For example, it is impossible to know the size of a market for a new drug without knowing whether the drug works on animals or on humans. Therefore, the technical development of the drug needs to occur before one can evaluate the market for it. Analyses of discounted cash flow based on net present value does not permit this sequential evaluation, requiring entrepreneurs to make their evaluations on the basis of assumptions about factors that are truly unknown, making those evaluations pure guess work.

Given these problems with the analysis of discounted cash flow based on net present value, a better approach to making decisions about new ventures is to examine them as real options. By treating a new venture as a series of steps and analyzing the value of making an investment in one step on the potential to make a future investment in another step, you will be better able to make the decisions that you need to make to evaluate a business opportunity.

One reason that real options are more effective than net present value calculations in evaluating new venture opportunities is that technology development occurs in an evolutionary fashion that lends itself to staged evaluation. For instance, in the typical technology development scenario, initial research results in the invention of a new technology, which then leads to the need for product development, which then results in the need for manufacturing, which then leads to the need for marketing. Because several things are unknown at each stage and will only become known if the venture passes through the previous stage, you cannot estimate all steps at once. Instead, they can only estimate the effect of one stage on the next stage.

Figure 10.1 illustrates that the results of real options analysis differ from traditional net present value calculations of discounted cash flows. As the figure indicates, real options can result in calculations of lower expected value than risk adjusted discounted cash flows. Why? Because options analysis requires decision making over time as information is revealed, rather than all at one point in time. Therefore, you do not incorporate all calculations about the outcome of the investment in research and development and the decision to go to market.

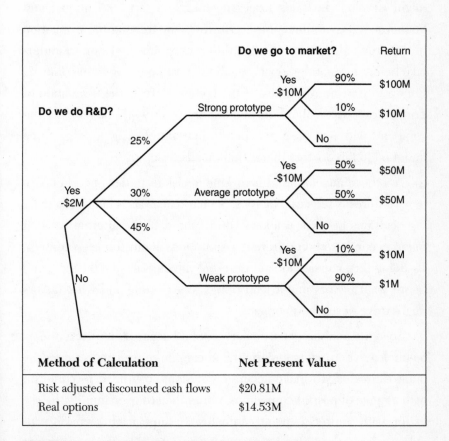

FIGURE 10.1   An Example of Real Options Evaluation

Instead, you only incorporate the calculations about the most favorable outcome in each stage and then decide from there whether to move forward. In this case, options analysis would suggest that you not move forward with a project that you otherwise might pursue.

Another reason that the use of real options is valuable to entrepreneurs is that they help entrepreneurs to maintain flexibility and avoid committing valuable resources to the development of a market that cannot be exploited with a particular new product. For example, a biotechnology start-up may not know if it should pursue the human or veterinary market for its new drug until it has conducted some tests on the efficacy of the drug on humans and animals. If the company does not evaluate product development by using real options, it might develop the sales forces necessary to tap both animal and human markets simultaneously. However, by treating the evaluation of the drug's efficacy on the two different groups as a step to undertake before evaluating how to reach the customer base, the company can avoid wasting resources. If the company treats the evaluation of drug efficacy as a real option, and the drug only works on animals, the company will not have to spend time developing a sales force designed to tap doctors that it then needs to scrap.

Another financial tool for making decisions under uncertainty in new ventures is scenario analysis. Scenario analysis is helpful in making decisions because it allows you to simulate the alternatives that might occur, based on different assumptions about the key variables. By doing this, you can look at different dimensions of a business and figure what factors might lead things to go wrong and what factors might drive desired outcomes.

Scenario analysis is particularly useful because the future of new technology ventures is uncertain and cannot be well represented by point estimates. To make accurate decisions, you need to come up with a range of possible outcomes, rather than to oversimplify the situation with imprecise point estimates. Because each scenario provides information about an expected outcome under different assumptions, scenario analysis allows you to avoid reliance on the inaccurate simplification of point estimates.

Moreover, accurate decision making is facilitated by the identification of the key assumptions that drive results. By examining scenarios, you can see what variables change the most in response to changes in key assumptions and which factors vary with changes in other factors. This information will help you to make plans that minimize the likelihood that adverse outcomes will happen and maximize the likelihood that beneficial results will occur.

One further point is worth making about scenario and options analyses. Successful entrepreneurs know that these tools are complements rather than substitutes. Therefore, they often use them together to make decisions about new ventures. When information is not completely known about alternatives, options analysis helps to make decisions about different alternatives over time, and scenario analysis helps to make decisions about different alternatives at a given point in time.

How Do Entrepreneurs Convince Stakeholders to Bear Risk?

The previous discussion raises the question of how you can convince stakeholders to bear risk for you, given that getting others to bear risks is sometimes a valuable strategy for entrepreneurs. The answer

Stop! Don't Do It!

1. Don't use standard net present value calculations to make decisions about new technology ventures.
2. Don't forget to investigate different scenarios when making decisions about your new venture.

is a function of several things, one of which is sharing rewards fairly. People bear risk because they get some sort of reward from it. Therefore, successful entrepreneurs share equity with people who bear some of their risk. Unsuccessful technology entrepreneurs want something for nothing. They do want to bear risk, but they refuse to share equity with those who would bear risks for them.[12]

Successful entrepreneurs honor implicit and explicit contracts. Stakeholders do not like to bear risk for entrepreneurs if they believe that entrepreneurs will opportunistically renegotiate the terms of their contracts once the risk is gone. They want entrepreneurs to maintain the division of equity that they agreed to when setting up the venture. So you can get others to bear risk for you by showing that you will adhere to the terms of your agreements even when you have the opportunity to renegotiate those terms in your favor.[13]

Successful entrepreneurs maintain commitment to their ventures. Other stakeholders do not like to bear risk for entrepreneurs if those entrepreneurs will not stick with their ventures. The fear of other stakeholders is that they will be left holding the bag for entrepreneurs who have moved on to other things. Therefore, a demonstration of commitment to your venture will be important if you want to maintain the support of stakeholders who bear risk for you.[14]

Successful entrepreneurs have social relationships with the stakeholders that bear risk for them. These social relationships make the stakeholders trust them and feel more comfortable bearing the risk. As was discussed in the last chapter, social relationships make entrepreneurs act less opportunistically toward the stakeholders in their ventures, as well as provide effective mechanisms for stakeholders to control entrepreneurs' behavior. As a result, raising money from people with whom you have a social relationship will make it more likely that those people will bear some of your risk for you.

Successful entrepreneurs bring together different parties at the same time, rather than sequentially. For instance, you might tell a supplier that a customer is on board and tell a customer that a sup-

Stop! Don't Do It!

1. Don't try to convince stakeholders to bear your risk for you without sharing rewards, honoring contracts, and maintaining commitment.

2. Don't approach your customers and suppliers sequentially; do it simultaneously.

plier is on board as a way to get both to commit to the venture. Doing this helps to get stakeholders to bear risk because it leads each stakeholder to believe that the other stakeholders are already on board. Therefore, they perceive their commitment as less risky than it actually is.[15] In general, you will be more successful at getting other people to bear your risk for you if you approach suppliers and customers this way when you seek to obtain resources for your new venture.

Successful entrepreneurs engage in a process of getting stakeholders to escalate their commitment. How do they do this? By getting each stakeholder to make a small commitment to the venture. Then they ask each stakeholder to make small increases in their commitments until those commitments reach the desired level. Because the stakeholders are asked to make only small increases in their com-

Questions to Ask Yourself

1. What can I do to reduce the risk inherent in my new venture?

2. What can I do to reallocate risk to other parties better able to bear it than me?

3. What can I do to reduce perceptions of the risk of my venture?

4. How can I analyze my investment decisions in a way that helps me to manage risk?

5. What can I do to convince stakeholders to bear some of the risk of my venture?

mitments each time, they are more willing to accept those increases, even when they might refuse if asked to make the overall commitment in one step.[16] In general, you will be more successful at getting other people to bear your risk for you if you escalate the commitment of your stakeholders when you seek to obtain resources from them for your new venture.

Summary

This chapter explained that new ventures face technical, market, and competitive uncertainties that require you to undertake risk management activities. You can reduce the risk that your new venture faces by searching for additional information, minimizing the magnitude of investments, and by maintaining flexibility. You can reallocate risks to those parties better able to manage risk or who seek risk. This includes such actions as transferring risk to diversified investors, reallocating risk to experienced or specialized stakeholders better able to manage it, shifting risk to those parties for whom the activities are less risky, and shifting risks to risk seekers. You can also manage risk by legitimating your new venture. You can do this by obtaining endorsements from representatives of the status quo, adhering to established rules and norms, and by engaging in collective action.

Successful entrepreneurs use two financial tools to evaluate opportunities: real options and scenario analysis. Real options help to make accurate decisions under uncertainty by not requiring the evaluation of things that are truly unknown and by permitting evaluation in successive stages. Scenario analysis helps to make accurate decisions by allowing evaluation in terms of ranges rather than point estimates and by allowing the identification of key assumptions about the relationships between variables.

Successful entrepreneurs convince stakeholders to bear some of the risk of their ventures. They do this by displaying attributes associated with successful entrepreneurs, by approaching customers and suppliers simultaneously, and by escalating commitment in a step-by-step manner.

Now that you understand all 10 rules of technology entrepreneurship, we now turn to some thoughts on how to bring them all together, which is the subject of the final chapter.

CONCLUSIONS

This book offered ten rules for you to follow to develop a business idea that can provide the basis for a successful high technology company. Each of these rules was explained in a different chapter of the book. The rules were

1. Select the right industry.

2. Identify valuable opportunities.

3. Manage technological transitions.

4. Identify and satisfy real market needs.

5. Understand customer adoption and market dynamics.

6. Exploit established company weaknesses.

7. Manage intellectual property effectively.

8. Create barriers to imitation.

9. Choose the right organizational form.

10. Manage risk and uncertainty effectively.

Below I summarize the things that you should do to follow these ten rules:

Rule Number 1: Select the Right Industry. You will be more successful if you select the right industry in which to start your company. The right industries for technology entrepreneurs are ones that are young and have not converged on a dominant design. They have simple production processes; low levels of new knowledge; a locus of innovation that lies outside the value chain; a lack of importance of complementary assets in marketing and distribution; large, growing, and segmented markets; a production process that is not capital or advertising intensive; productive activity that is not concentrated in a small number of firms; and small average firm size.

Rule Number 2: Identify valuable opportunities. You will be more successful if you identify valuable opportunities. This means that you should identify the source of the opportunity be it technological change, political/regulatory change, social/demographic change, or change in industrial structure. You should figure out the form that the efforts to exploit the opportunity will take. You should match the opportunity to specific types of innovation. You need to identify where in the innovation chain the change occurs. You also need to understand how individuals identify opportunities.

Rule Number 3: Manage technological transitions. You will be more successful if you understand the evolutionary patterns of technological development. This means

- Recognizing the role of new firms in shifting technology S-curves

- Understanding dominant designs and how they influence competition by new and established firms in an industry

- Considering the role of technical standards in technological evolution

- Managing the differences in the development of increasing and decreasing returns business

Rule Number 4: Identify and satisfy real market needs. You will be more successful if you identify and satisfy real market needs than if you do not. In addition, you will be more successful if you evaluate customer preferences in a way that is effective for new products and services, which often means using techniques other than focus groups and surveys. Furthermore, you will be more successful if your products and services meet customer needs in an economic manner and in a way that is better than the approach offered by the competition. Finally, you will be more successful if you rely on personal selling and get the prices for new products right.

Rule Number 5: Understand customer adoption and market dynamics. You will be more successful if you understand customer adoption, which tends to follow an S-shaped pattern. Moreover, you will be more successful if you adapt your products to the demands of mainstream customers, and focus on the right target market to transition to the majority of customers. Furthermore, you will be more successful if you understand market dynamics, which means avoiding static estimation of markets, and understanding technology diffusion and substitution.

Rule Number 6: Exploit established company weaknesses. You will be more successful if you exploit established company weaknesses, rather than challenging their strengths. Most of the time established companies succeed in competition with new firms because they have the advantages of the learning curve, reputation, existing cash flow, scale economies, and complementary assets in marketing and manufacturing. However, established firms have weaknesses that you can exploit, including a focus on the efficiency of existing operations, generating value from current capabilities, the need to satisfy existing customers, existing organizational structures that constrain communication patterns and information flow, a need to reward people for doing their existing jobs, and hierarchies to manage their existing operations. You also will be more successful if you exploit uncertain, discrete, general purpose technologies embedded in human capital, rather than certain, systemic, single-purpose technologies embedded in physical capital.

Rule Number 7: Manage intellectual property effectively. You will be more successful if you deter imitation of your new products and services, which are easy for large, established companies to imitate most of the time. This can be done through two alternative means: secrecy and patenting. Secrecy is most effective when there are few alternative sources of information other than the entrepreneur, the product or service is complex, limited numbers of people would be able to make use of information about the process of creating the new product or service in such a way as to be able to replicate it, the knowledge necessary to create the product or service is tacit, and the process by which the product or service created is poorly understood.

Patenting is an important tool because it allows you to assemble the value chain necessary to produce and distribute your new product before competitors can imitate it. However, patents have several limitations: they are possible to obtain for only a small number of types of products or services, require the new product to be a significant improvement over prior art, are often ineffective alone, are expensive, are not always very strong, require disclosure of the invention, and are not very effective in many industries.

Rule Number 8: Create barriers to imitation. You will be more successful if your create barriers to imitation through the control of resources, building brand-name reputations, exploiting learning curves, developing first mover advantages, and controlling complementary assets in manufacturing and marketing. Controlling resources is most effective when there is a bottleneck in the production process, making one resource crucial and rare. Establishing a reputation is rarely effective for entrepreneurs because advertising takes time to work, and is subject to economies of scale. Exploiting the learning curve is most effective when a new firm is an early entrant in an industry and when the knowledge gained from experience is proprietary. Being the first mover is an advantage when network externalities exist and when real or psychological switching costs are high. Exploiting complementary assets is most effective when patent protection in an industry is weak, and the industry has converged on a dominant design. However, this strategy is rarely effective for entrepreneurs because they almost never have complementary assets in place at the time of their formation, and because these assets are often specialized, making it difficult to contract for them.

Rule Number 9: Choose the right organizational form. You will be more successful if you do not always exploit opportunities by owning all parts of the value chain, but instead match the organizational form to the opportunity you are seeking to pursue. This means employing contractual modes of opportunity exploitation, such as licensing, franchising, and strategic alliances, when opportunities are expensive to exploit; when you need to exploit opportunities quickly; when you lack the capabilities to exploit the opportunities yourself; when the technologies that you are exploiting are discrete, based on codified knowledge, are subject to technical standards, and are linked to nonspecialized complementary assets; and when the information problems of employee adverse selection and shirking are dominant.

Rule Number 10: Manage risk and uncertainty effectively. You will be more successful if you reduce the risk that your new venture faces, which you can do by searching for additional information, minimizing the magnitude of investments, and by maintaining flexibility. You will also be more successful if you reallocate risks to those parties best able to manage it, as is done by shifting risks to risk seekers, to diversified investors, to experienced or specialized stakeholders and to those parties for whom the activities are less risky. You will be more successful if you manage the perceptions of the risk of your venture by obtaining endorsements from representatives of the status quo, adhering to established rules and norms, and by engaging in collective action. Finally, you will be more successful if you use two financial tools to evaluate opportunities: real options and scenario analysis.

A Final Comment

Of the vast numbers of people who start high technology companies in the United States every year, only a few are very successful. Most of these founders of new high technology companies end up with failed ventures and no financial returns to show for all of their effort. However, every year a small number of people start truly successful technology companies that often go public and generate tremendous riches for them and most everyone involved with their ventures. While the odds of being very successful are not great, that doesn't mean that entrepreneurs are powerless to improve their chances of being among the small number of success stories.

This book explained that being a successful entrepreneur is much like being a good professional gambler. If you know the games where the odds are least stacked in favor of the house, and you understand the rules of the game you are playing, you can greatly improve your chances of winning. Following the rules outlined in the book will help you to identify the fertile ground—a truly extraordinary business opportunity that will foster the development of a new high-technology company. While this information will not guarantee your success, it will increase your odds dramatically.

Now that you know the rules of the technology entrepreneurship game, you are ready to play. Good luck.

NOTES

Introduction

1. P. Reynolds and S. White, *The Entrepreneurial Process: Economic Growth, Men, Women and Minorities* (Westport, CT: Quorum Books,1997).

2. B. Hamilton, "Does Entrepreneurship Pay? An Empirical analysis of the Returns to Self-employment." *Journal of Political Economy* 108 no. 3(2000): 604–31.

3. Ibid.

Chapter 1

1. F. Malerba and L. Orsenigo, "Technological Regimes and Sectoral Patterns of Innovative Activities." *Industrial and Corporate Change* 6 (1997): 83–117.

2. Ibid.

3. J. Eckhardt, *Industry Differences in Entrepreneurial Opportunities,* Ph.D. diss., University of Maryland, 2002.

4. D. Audretsch and Z. Acs, "New Firm Startups, Technology, and Macroeconomic Fluctuations." *Small Business Economics* 6 (1994): 439–49.

5. J. Mata and P. Portugal, "Life Duration of New Firms." *Journal of Industrial Economics* 42 no. 3 (1994): 227–43.

6. W. Barnett, "The Dynamics of Competitive Intensity." *Administrative Science Quarterly,* 42 (1997): 128–60.

7. G. Moore, *Crossing the Chasm* (New York: Harper Collins, 1991).

8. J. Utterback, *Mastering the Dynamics of Innovation.* (Cambridge: Harvard Business School Press, 1994).

9. Ibid.

10. D. Audretsch, "New Firm Survival and the Technological Regime." *Review of Economics and Statistics* (1991): 441–50.

11. S. Shane, A *General Theory of Entrepreneurship: The Individual-Opportunity Nexus* (Cheltenham, UK: Edward Elgar, 2003).

12. K. Eisenhardt and K. Schoonhoven. "Organizational Growth: Linking Founding Team, Strategy, Environment, and Growth among U.S. Semiconductor Ventures, 1978–1988." *Administrative Science Quarterly* 35 (1990): 504–29.

13. D. Audretsch and T. Mahmood, T. "The Hazard Rate of New Establishments." *Economic Letters,* 36 (1991): 409–12.

14. Z. Acs and D. Audretsch, "Small Firm Entry in U.S. Manufacturing." *Economica* (1989): 255–66.

Chapter 2

1. J. A. Schumpeter, *The Theory of Economic Development: An Inquiry into Profits, Capital Credit, Interest, and the Business Cycle.* (Cambridge, MA: Harvard University Press, 1934).

2. S. Shane, "Explaining Variation in Rates of Entrepreneurship in the United States: 1899–1988." *Journal of Management* 22 no. 5 (1996): 747–81.

3. T. Holmes and J. Schmitz, "A Gain from Trade: From Unproductive to Productive Entrepreneurship." *Journal of Monetary Economics* 47 (2001): 417–46.

4. M. Feldman, "The Entrepreneurial Event Revisited: Firm Formation in a Regional Context." *Industrial and Corporate Change,* 10 no. 4 (2001): 861–91.

5. Schumpteter, J. *The Theory of Economic Development.* op. cit.

6. Mansfield, E. "How Rapidly Does Technology Leak Out?" *Journal of Industrial Economics,* 34 no. 2 (1985): 217–23.

7. A. Klevorick, R. Levin, R. Nelson, and S. Winter, "On the Sources of Significance of Inter-industry Differences in Technological Opportunities." *Research Policy* 24 (1995): 185–205.

8. Ibid.

9. Ibid.

10. Ibid.

11. I. Kirzner, "Entrepreneurial Discovery and the Competitive Market Process: An Austrian Approach." *Journal of Economic Literature* 35 (1997): 60–85.

12. D. Blanchflower and A. Oswald, "What Makes an Entrepreneur?" *Journal of Labor Economics,* 16 (1998): 26–60.

13. S. Shane, *A General Theory of Entrepreneurship: The Individual-Opportunity Nexus* (Cheltenham, U.K.: Edward Elgar, 2003).

14. Ibid.
15. D. Sarasvathy, H. Simon, and L. Lave, "Perceiving and Managing Business Risks: Differences between Entrepreneurs and Bankers." *Journal of Economic Behavior and Organization*, 33 (1998): 207–25.
16. Ibid.
17. K. Hyrsky and A. Kangasharju, "Adapters and Innovators in Non-urban Environment," in *Frontiers of Entrepreneurship Research*, ed. P. Reynolds, W. Bygrave, N., Carter, S. Manigart, C. Mason, G. Meyer, and K. Shaver (Babson Park: MA Babson College, 1998).
18. S. Shane, *A General Theory of Entrepreneurship*. op. cit.

Chapter 3

1. G. Dosi, "Sources, Procedures, and Microeconomic Effects of Innovation." *Journal of Economic Literature*, 26 (1988): 1120–71.
2. R. Foster, *Innovation: The Attacker's Advantage* (New York: Summit Books, 1986).
3. Ibid.
4. Ibid.
5. Ibid.
6. J. Utterback, *Mastering the Dynamics of Innovation* (Cambridge: Harvard Business School Press, 1994).
7. Ibid.
8. Ibid.
9. S. Klepper and E. Graddy, "The Evolution of New Industries and the Determinants of Market Structure." *Rand Journal of Economics*, 21 no. 1 (1990): 32.
10. D. Kirsch, *Electric Vehicles and the Burden of History* (New Brunswick, NJ: Rutgers University Press, 2000).
11. Ibid.
12. J. Utterback, *Mastering the Dynamics of Innovation*. op. cit.
13. P. David, "Clio and the Economics of QWERTY." American Economic Review 75 (1985): 332–37.
14. P. Tam, "Cloud over Sun Microsystems: Plummeting Computer Prices." *Wall Street Journal*, 242 no. 76 (2003): A1, A16.
15. B. Arthur, "Increasing Returns and the New World of Business." *Harvard Business Review* (July–August 1996): 100–109.
16. M. Cusumano, Y. Mylonadis, and R. Rosenbloom, "Strategic Maneuvering and Mass Market Dynamics: The Triumph of VHS over Beta." *Business History Review* 66 (1992): 51–94.
17. B. Arthur, "Increasing Returns and the New World of Business." op. cit.
18. Ibid.
19. Ibid.

Chapter 4

1. D. Barton, *Commercializing Technology: Imaginative Understanding of User Needs* (Boston MA: Harvard Business School Note 9-694-102, 1994).
2. A. Bhide, *Selling as a Systematic Process* (Boston, MA: Harvard Business School Note 9-935-091, 1994).
3. Ibid.
4. Ibid.

Chapter 5

1. E. Rogers, *Diffusion of Innovations* (New York: Free Press, 1983).
2. G. Moore, *Crossing the Chasm* (New York: Harper Collins, 1991).
3. E. Rogers, *Diffusion of Innovations*. op. cit.
4. G. Moore, *Crossing the Chasm*. op. cit.
5. Ibid.
6. Ibid.
7. Ibid.
8. Ibid.
9. Ibid.
10. Ibid.
11. Ibid.
12. L. Girfalco, *Dynamics of Technological Change* (New York: Van Nostrand, 1991).
13. Ibid.
14. Rogers, *Diffusion of Innovations*. op. cit.
15. Ibid.
16. Ibid.
17. Girfalco, *Dynamics of Technological Change*. op. cit.
18. Rogers, *Diffusion of Innovations*. op. cit.
19. Girfalco, *Dynamics of Technological Change*. op. cit.
20. Ibid.

Chapter 6

1. H. Aldrich, *Organizations Evolving* (London: Sage, 1999).
2. D. Teece, "Profiting from Technological Innovation: Implications for Integration, Collaboration, Licensing and Public Policy," in D. Teece (ed), *The Competitive Challenge*, ed. D. Teece (Cambridge, MA: Ballinger, 1987).

3. C. Christiansen, *The Innovator's Dilemma* (Cambridge: Harvard Business School Press, 1997).

4. Ibid.

5. P. Grant, and A. Latour, "Battered Telecoms Face New Challenge: Internet Calling," *Wall Street Journal*, October 9, 2003, pp. A1, A9.

6. C. Christiansen, *The Innovator's Dilemma*. op. cit.

7. R. Henderson and K. Clark, "Architectural Innovation: The Reconfiguration of Existing Product Technologies and the Failure of Established Firms. *Administrative Science Quarterly* 35 (1990): 9–30.

8. Ibid.

9. B. Holmstrom, "Agency Costs and Innovation." *Journal of Economic Behavior and Organization* 12 (1989): 305–27.

10. R. Kanter, "When a Thousand Flowers Bloom: Structural, Collective, and Social Conditions for Innovations in Organization." *Research in Organizational Behavior* 10 (1988): 169–211.

11. D. Barton, *Commercializing Technology: Imaginative Understanding of User Needs* (Boston, MA: Harvard Business School Note 9-694-102, 1994).

12. S. Winter, "Schumpeterian Competition in Alternative Technological Regimes." *Journal of Economic Behavior and Organization* (1984): 287–320.

13. R. Young and J. Francis, "Entrepreneurship and Innovation in Small Manufacturing Firms," *Social Science Quarterly* 72 no. 1 (1991): 149–62.

Chapter 7

1. R. Levin, A. Klevorick, R. Nelson, and S. Winter, "Appropriating the Returns from Industrial Research and Development." *Brookings Papers on Economic Activity* 3 (1987): 783–832.

2. E. Mansfield, "How Rapidly Does Industrial Technology Leak Out?" *Journal of Industrial Economics* 34 no. 2 (1985): 217–23.

3. R. Levin, A. Klevorick, R. Nelson, and S. Winter, "Appropriating the Returns from Industrial Research and Development." op. cit.

4. Ibid.

5. Ibid.

6. S. Shane, *A General Theory of Entrepreneurship: The Individual-Opportunity Nexus* (Cheltenham, U.K.: Edward Elgar, 2003).

7. Ibid.

8. R. Nelson, and S. Winter, *An Evolutionary Theory of Economic Change* (Cambridge, MA: Belknap Press, 1982).

9. L. Zucker, M. Darby, and M. Brewer, "Intellectual Human Capital and the Birth of U.S. Biotechnology Enterprises. *American Economic Review* 88 no. 1 (1998): 290–305.

10. U.S. Department of Commerce. *General Information Concerning Patents* (Washington, DC: U.S. Government Printing Office, 1992).

11. Ibid.

12. O. Fuerst, and U. Geiger, *From Concept to Wall Street: A Complete Guide to Entrepreneurship and Venture Capital* (New York: Financial Times Prentice Hall, 2003).

13. D. Debelak, "Patent Lather," www.entrepreneur.com/article/ 0,4621,274473,00.html (accessed 2000).

14. L. Gomes, "Though a Trailblazer, Is Tivo Overreaching in Its Patent Claims?" *Wall Street Journal,* February 9, 2004, p. B1.

15. R. Levin, A. Klevorick, R. Nelson, and S. Winter, "Appropriating the Returns from Industrial Research and Development." op. cit.

16. Ibid.

17. Ibid.

18. Ibid.

Chapter 8

1. W. Cohen, R. Nelson, and J. Walsh, "Protecting Their Intellectual Assets: Appropriability Conditions and Why U.S. Manufacturing Firms Patent (or Not)." *NBER Working Paper,* No. 7552, 2000.

2. Ibid.

3. S. Shane, *A General Theory of Entrepreneurship: The Individual-Opportunity Nexus.* (Cheltenham, U.K.: Edward Elgar, 2003).

4. R. Levin, A. Klevorick, R. Nelson, and S. Winter, "Appropriating the Returns from Industrial Research and Development." *Brookings Papers on Economic Activity* 3 (1987): 783–832.

5. C. Shapiro, H. Varian, "The Art of Standard Wars." *California Management Review* (winter 1999): 8–32

6. K. Sandberg, "Rethinking the First Mover Advantage." *Harvard Management Update* 6 no. 5 (2001): 1–4.

7. R. Kerin, P. Varadarajan, and R. Peterson, "First Mover Advantage: A Synthesis, Conceptual Framework, and Research Propositions." *Journal of Marketing* 56 (1993): 33–52.

8. M. Mellahi, and M. Johnson, "Does It Pay to Be a First Mover in E.commerce?" *Management Decision* 38 no. 7 (2000): 445–52.

9. D. Teece, "Profiting from Technological Innovation: Implications for Integration, Collaboration, Licensing and Public Policy," in *The Competitive Challenge*, ed. D. Teece (Cambridge, MA: Ballinger, 1987).

10. Ibid.

11. Ibid.

12. Ibid.

13. Ibid.

14. Ibid.

15. Ibid.

Chapter 9

1. S. Venkataraman, "The Distinctive Domain of Entrepreneurship Research: An Editor's Perspective," in *Advances in Entrepreneurship, Firm Emergence, and Growth,* J. Katz and R. Brockhaus, ed. 3: 119–38 (Greenwich, CT: JAI Press, 1997).

2. D. Evans, and L. Leighton, "Some Empirical Aspects of Entrepreneurship." *American Economic Review* 79 (1989): 519–35.

3. D. Teece, "Profiting from Technological Innovation: Implications for Integration, Collaboration, Licensing, and Public Policy" *Research Policy,* 15 (1986): 286–305.

4. H. Chesborough and D. Teece, "When is Virtual Virtuous?" *Harvard Business Review* (January–February): 65–73.

5. D. Audretsch, "Technological Regimes, Industrial Demography and the Evolution of Industrial Structures." *Industrial and Corporate Change* 6 (1997): 49–82.

6. H. Chesborough and D. Teece. "When Is Virtual Virtuous?" op. cit.

7. Ibid.

8. K. Arrow, "Economic Welfare and the Allocation of Resources for Inventions," in *The Rate and Direction of Inventive Activity,* ed. R. Nelson (Princeton, NJ: Princeton University Press, 1962).

9. S. Shane, "Making New Franchise Systems Work." *Strategic Management Journal,* 19 no. 7 (1998): 697–707.

10. Ibid.

11. P. Azoulay and S. Shane, "Entrepreneurs, Contracts and the Failure of Young Firms." *Management Science,* 47 no. 3 (2001): 337–58.

Chapter 10

1. F. Delmar and S. Shane, "Does Business Planning Facilitate the Development of New Ventures." *Strategic Management Journal* 24 (2003): 1165–1185.

2. A. Bhide and H. Stevenson, "Attracting Stakeholders," in *The Entrepreneurial Venture,* ed. W. Sahlman and H. Stevenson: 149–59. (Boston: Harvard Business School Press, 1992),

3. E. Roberts, *Entrepreneurs in High Technology* (New York: Oxford University Press, 1991).

4. R. Caves, "Industrial Organization and New Findings on the Turnover and Mobility of Firms." *Journal of Economic Literature* 36 (1998): 1947–82.

5. C. Christiansen and J. Bower, "Customer Power, Strategic Investment, and the Failure of Leading Firms." *Strategic Management Journal* 17 (1996): 197–218.

6. Bhide and Stevenson, "Attracting Stakeholders." op. cit.

7. Ibid.

8. H. Rao, "The Social Construction of Reputation: Certification Contests, Legitimation and the Survival of Organizations in the American Automobile Industry: 1895–1912." *Strategic Management Journal* 13 (1994): 29–44.

9. Ibid.

10. J. Starr and I. MacMillan, "Resource Cooptation via Social Contracting: Resource Acquisition Strategies for New Ventures." *Strategic Management Journal* 11 (1990): 79–92.

11. H. Aldrich, *Organizations Evolving* (London: Sage, 1999).

12. A. Bhide and H. Stevenson, "Attracting Stakeholders." op. cit.

13. Ibid.

14. Ibid.

15. Ibid.

16. Ibid.

LIST OF ACKNOWLEDGMENTS FOR TABLES AND FIGURES

Table1.1: Percent of Firms in Selected Industries That Have Become Inc 500 Firms. Source: Adapted from data contained in Eckhardt, J. 2003. *When the Weak Acquire Wealth: An Examination of the Distribution of High Growth Startups in the U.S. Economy.* Ph.D. diss., University of Maryland.

Figure 3.1: The S-shaped Curve of Technology Development. Source: Adapted from Foster, R. 1986. *Innovation: The Attacker's Advantage* (New York: Summit Books).

Figure 5.1: The Normal Distribution of Product Adoption. Source: Adapted from Rogers, E. 1983. *Diffusion of Innovations* (New York: Free Press), p. 247.

Figure 5.2: Crossing the Chasm. Source: Adapted from Moore, G. 1991. *Crossing the Chasm.* (New York: Harper Collins), p. 17.

Figure 5.3:   The S-Shaped Curve of Diffusion. Source: Adapted
               from Rogers, S. 1983. *Diffusion of Innovations.* (New
               York: Free Press), p. 243.

Figure 6.1:   An Example of the Effect of the Learning Curve on
               Production Rates. Source: Adapted from Baron, R.,
               and Shane, S. 2005. *Entrepreneurship: A Process
               Perspective* (Mason, Ohio: Southwestern), p. 41.

Table 7.1:   Effectiveness of Product Patents by Industry. Source:
               Adapted from Levin, R., Klevorick, A., Nelson, R., and
               Winter, S. 1987. Appropriating the returns to industrial
               research and development. *Brookings Papers on
               Economic Activity* 3, p. 797.

Figure 10.1:   An Example of Real Options Evaluation. Source:
               Adapted from Afuah, A. 1998. *Innovation Manage-
               ment: Strategies, Implementation and Profits* (New
               York: Oxford University Press), p. 209.

INDEX

A

Accelerating the pace to market,
165–166
Adoption
customer, 81–99
of a dominant design, 12–13
of new products, 11
Advertising
brand-name, 150–151
intensity, 14–15
Amazon.com, 25, 110
ARPANET, 31
Assets, complementary, 105–106
Average firm size, importance of, 16

B

Barnes & Noble, 109–110
Brand-name, 14
Brand-name reputation, 150–151
costs relative to, 151
Broadband Internet, 54
Business plan, developing, 180

C

Capital intensity, 14
Capturing the returns from introducing
new products, 147–162

complementary assets, 156–161
establishing a reputation,
150–152
first mover advantage, 154–156
learning curve advantage in, 152
obtaining control over resources,
148–149
Cash flow, 104
discounted, 190
Change
in industry structure, 24–25
political and regulatory, 22–23
technological, 20–22
Choosing the right organizational form,
163–175
accelerating the pace to market,
165–166
contractual modes of opportunity
exploitation, 165–167, 168,
173
cost of exploitation, 164
hierarchical modes of opportunity
exploitation, 163, 167–168
making use of the best capabilities,
166–167
managing information problems in
organizing, 170–174

Choosing the right organizational form
  (*cont.*)
  market-based modes of opportunity
      exploitation, 164–165, 168, 169
  nature of the technology, 167–170
Closing a sale, 76
Coca-Cola, 130, 133
Codification of knowledge, 6
Complementary assets, 105–106,
      156–161
  importance of, 158
  mechanism for capturing returns to
      new product introduction,
      156–161
Complex production process, 4–5
Concentration, 15
Contracts, 168
Contractual modes of opportunity
      exploitation, 165–167, 168, 173
Convincing stakeholders to bear risk,
      193–196
Copyrights, 135
Cost
  advertising, 15
  of brand-name reputation, 151
  drug production, 53
  fixed, 183
  of opportunity exploitation, 164–165
  patenting, 139–140
  of producing software, 53
  of switching products, 54, 55
  of technological change, 21
  variable, 183
Customer
  demand, 8–10
  lock in, 55–56
  needs, identifying and satisfying,
      64–66
  preferences, gathering information
      about, 66–69
  requirements, in the selling process, 76
Customer adoption, 11, 81–99
  capturing the majority of the market,
      85–87
  market dynamics and, 89–97
  pattern of, understanding, 82–85
  selecting the right customers, 87–89

D
Decreasing returns, 52
Demand, shift in, 24

Demand conditions, 8–10
  aspects of, 8–9
Demographic trend, 24
Deregulation, opportunities for new
      business, 22
Development, evolutionary patterns of,
      41–42
Diffusion patterns, 91–97
Disclosure paradox, 170
Disclosure problems, 171
Discounted cash flow, 190
Discreteness, 117–118
DISH Network, patent claim, 141
Dominant designs
  adoption of, 12–13
  characteristics, 48–49
  factors that lead to, 48
  role of, 46–49

E
eBay, 54, 155
E-books, 45
Economical solution to real customer
      needs, 71–73
Endorsement, 187
Established companies' advantages,
      102–106
  cash flow, 104
  complementary assets, 105–106
  learning curve, 102–103
  reputation, 103–104
  scale economies, 104–105
Established companies' weaknesses,
      exploiting, 106–116
  constraints of organizational
      structure, 113–114
  exploiting existing capabilities,
      108–111
  focus on efficiency, 107
  need to reward employees,
      114–115
  need to satisfy existing customers,
      111–113
  product development in a
      bureaucracy, difficulty of,
      115–116
Estimating market size. *see* Market
      dynamics
Ethernet, 30
Evolutionary patterns of development,
      41–42

F

First mover advantage, 54–55,
        154–156
Fixed costs, 183
Flexibility, maintaining, 184–185
Forms of opportunities: beyond new
        products or services, 25–27
Franchising, 171–172
Free riding, 172

G

Gathering information about customer
        preferences, 66–69
    market research, 69–70
General Motors, 156
General purpose, 118–119

H

Hidden costs, 77–78
Hierarchical modes of opportunity
        exploitation, 163, 167–168
High fixed costs, 77
Human capital intensity, 118
Hyundai, 156

I

Identifying and satisfying real market
        needs, 63–80
    gathering information about
        customer preferences, 66–69
    necessities, nice to haves, and the
        unnecessary, distinguishing,
        70–71
    offering better alternatives then
        competition, 73–74
    understanding the marketing and
        selling process, 75–79
Identifying valuable opportunities,
        19–38
    access to information, 32–33
    forms of opportunities: beyond new
        products or services, 25–27
    information processing, effective,
        34–36
    matching innovation to types of
        opportunity, 27–29
    recognizing that an opportunity
        exists, 31–32
    sources of opportunities, 20–25
    understanding the innovation chain,
        29–31

Imitation
    of a documented process, 132
    legal barriers to, 135
    of new products or services,
        126–129
Inc 500, 2
Increasing returns businesses, 52–59
    and customer lock in, 55
    large bets in, 57–59
    open systems strategies in, 56–57
    software industry as example of, 53,
        55
    strategic partnering in, 57
    switching costs and, 54
Industry
    dimensions that affect performance
        of new firms, 4–16
    dynamics, effect of technological
        change on, 21–22
    life cycles, 11–13
    structure, 14–16, 24–25
        changes in, 24–25
Information
    access to, 32–33
    problems, managing, 170–174
    processing, effective, 34–36
    searching for, 179–181
Innovation, 6–7
    chain, importance of understanding,
        29–31
    relationship between opportunity
        and, 27–29
Innovators, 83
Intel, 7
Intellectual property, 125–145

K

Knowledge conditions, 4–8
    codification of knowledge, 6
    complexity of production process,
        4–5
    innovation, 6–7
    new knowledge creation, 5–6
Kodak, 110

L

Laggards, 84
Learning curve, 12, 102–103
    advantage of established companies,
        102–103

Learning curve (*cont.*)
  mechanism for capturing returns to
      new product introduction,
      152–153
Licensing, 166–167
Life cycles, industry, 11–13

M
Maintaining flexibility, 184–185
Majority, 83
  of the market, capturing, 85–87
Making use of the best capabilities,
      166–167
Managing information problems in
      organizing, 170–174
  disclosure problems, 170–171
Managing intellectual property,
      125–145
Managing risk and uncertainty,
      177–197
  convincing stakeholders to bear risk,
      193–196
  risk perception strategies, 186–188
  risk reallocation strategies,
      185–186
  risk reduction strategies, 179–185
  tools for, 188–193
Managing technological evolution,
      39–61
  evolutionary patterns of
      development, 41–42
  increasing returns businesses,
      52–59
  projecting Foster's S-curves, 42–46
  role of dominant designs, 46–49
  technical standards, role of, 49–52
Market-based modes of opportunity
      exploitation, 164–165, 168,
      169
Market dynamics, 89–97
  diffusion and substitution patterns,
      91–97
  static estimates, trap of, 89–91
Marketing process, 75–79
  pricing new products, 77–79
Microsoft, 49, 51
Minimizing investment, 182–184

N
Netscape, 31
Network externalities, 53

New firms
  industry dimensions that affect
      performance of, 4–16
  that become *Inc* 500 firms by
      industry, 3
Noncompete agreements, 7

O
Obtaining control over resources,
      148–149
Offering better alternatives then
      competition, 73–74
Open systems strategies, 56–57
Opportunities, sources of, 20–25
  changes in industry structure, 24–25
  political and regulatory change,
      22–23
  social and demographic change,
      23–24
  technological change, 20–22
Opportunities that favor new firms,
      117–121
  discreteness, 117–118
  general purpose, 118–119
  human capital intensity, 118
  uncertainty, 119–121
Opportunity
  exploitation, cost of, 164–165
  and innovation, relationship
      between, 27–29
  recognizing a valuable, 31–32
Opportunity exploitation
  contractual modes of, 165–167, 168,
      173
  hierarchical modes of, 163, 167–168
  market-based modes, 164–165, 168,
      169
Organizational form, 163–175

P
Patents, 134–144
  costs associated with, 139–140
  defined, 135
  disadvantage of, 142
  effectiveness by industry, 143
  importance of, 135–136
  limitation of, 136, 138
Perception, shift in, 24
Personal selling, importance of, 75–77
Pharmaceutical industry, 15
Political and regulatory change, 22–23

Pricing new products, 77–79
   affect of the environment on, 78
   factoring in production costs,
     77–78
Production process, complexity of, 4–5
Projecting customer adoption, 82–85

Q
QWERTY keyboard, 50

R
"Razor blade model," 55
Real customer needs
   developing an economical solution
     for, 71–73
   identifying, 64–65
   satisfying, 66
Real options, tool for managing
     uncertainty, 188–193
Recognizing a valuable opportunity,
     31–32
Reputation, 103–104
   brand-name, 150–151
   establishing a, 150–152
Resources, obtaining control over,
     148–149
Risk perception strategies, 186–188
Risk reallocation strategies, 185–186
Risk reduction strategies, 179–185
   maintaining flexibility, 184–185
   minimizing investment, 182–184
   searching for information, 179–181

S
Satisfying real customer needs, 66
Scale economies, 104–105
Scenario analysis, tool for managing
     uncertainty, 188–193
Searching for information, 179–181
Secrecy, 129–134
   effective use of, 130–131
   trade, 132–134
Segmented markets, 9–10
Selecting the right industry, 1–18
Selling process, 75–79
   closing the sale, 76
   customer requirements, 76
   generating customer interest, 75
   personal selling, importance of,
     75–77
Shift in perception, 24

Social and demographic change,
     23–24
   demographic trend, 24
   shift in perception, 24
   social trend, 23–24
Social trend, 23
Sony, 152
Sources of opportunities, 20–25
Specialized complementary assets, 159
S-shaped curve, 42–46
   defining, 42
   of diffusion, 92
   of technology development, 43
Stakeholders, convincing to bear risk,
     193–196
Static estimates, trap of, 89–91
Strategic alliances, 165, 187
Strategic partnering, 57
Structure, industry, 14–16
Substitution patterns, 91–97
Sun Microsystems, 50
Switching costs, 54, 155

T
Technical standards, role of, 49–52
Technological change, 20–22
   commercial viability of, 21
   cost of, 21
   effect on industry dynamics, 21–22
TiVo, patent claim, 141
Tools for managing risk and
     uncertainty, 188–193
Trademarks, 135
Trade secrets, 132–134

U
Uncertainty, 119–121
   tools for managing, 188–193

V
Variable costs, 183
Venture capitalists, 185
Voice-over Internet protocol, 22, 43,
     54, 110

W
Windows operating system, 49

X
Xerox Corporation, 30

ABOUT CONCENTRATED KNOWLEDGE CORPORATION
the producers of the CD enclosed in the back of this book

CKC invites you to learn more about receiving summaries of the best business books of the year delivered right to your door or computer.

There are so many great business books, but so little time. You know you need to keep current with the expanding base of knowledge. But how can you possibly keep up with all that reading?

The solution is *Soundview Executive Book Summaries.*®

Our experienced editors receive all the newly published business books and select the year's 30 best. These titles are condensed into 8-page print and 20-minute audio summaries – with the essential information you need to keep up. You'll quickly gain a working knowledge to prepare for presentations, make decisions, assume leadership responsibilities, and respond to high-pressure situations.

Gain the confidence that only such a broad scope of knowledge can provide by subscribing today. Call the number below or visit our Web site. You'll be happy you did.

Call 1-800-521-1227 (610-558-9495) or go to
www.summary.com/wp

SOUNDVIEW **Executive Book Summaries®**
A Concentrated Knowledge Corporation

ABOUT THE AUDIO CD

As you've probably already noticed, this book includes an audio CD in the back. This is a unique feature of Wharton School Publishing books, which sets these books apart from other business books in the market. This audio CD is included to give you a richer experience of the information that's included in the book itself.

Book Summary

On the audio CD you'll find a short 20-minute summary of the contents of the book, produced by Concentrated Knowledge Corporation. This summary will help you to quickly grasp the over-all thrust of the book and its major points. The summary can function as a pre-read to the book or as a review after you've finished. You can also pass this CD on to a friend who may be thinking about buying the book but needs more information.

Author Interview

The second feature of the CD is an interview between the book's author(s) and CKC's editor-in-chief. You can listen to the author(s) discuss his work in his own words, and hear his response to thought-provoking questions about the concepts introduced in the book.

We're confident that you'll find this audio content a complimentary partner to the text.

For more information about Concentrated Knowledge Corporation and its flagship publication Soundview Executive Book Summaries, go to www.summary.com/wp. You can also call them at 1-800-521-1227 (610-558-9495).

Limited Warranty

Wharton School Publishing warrants only that the media on which this audio CD is delivered shall be free from defects in material and workmanship under normal use for a period of thirty (30) days from the date of your purchase. Your only remedy, and Wharton School Publishing's only obligation, under this limited warranty is, at Wharton School Publishing's option, return of the warranted item for replacement. Any replacement of media under this warranty will not extend the original warranty period. The above warranty will not apply if Wharton School Publishing determines in good faith that the audio CD and/or the media has been subject to misuse, neglect, repair, alteration or damage by you. EXCEPT FOR THE ABOVE WARRANTY, WHARTON SCHOOL PUBLISHING DISCLAIMS ALL WARRANTIES, EXPRESS OR IMPLIED, INCLUDING, WITHOUT LIMITATION, THE IMPLIED WARRANTIES OF MERCHANTABILITY AND FITNESS FOR A PARTICULAR PURPOSE. SOME JURISDICTIONS DO NOT ALLOW THE LIMITATION OF IMPLIED WARRANTIES, SO THE ABOVE LIMITATIONS MAY NOT ALWAYS APPLY.

Technical Support

If this Audio CD is damaged, you may obtain a replacement copy by sending an email that describes the problem to: disc_exchange@prenhall.com. If you are having problems with this software, call 800-677-6337 between 8:00 a.m. and 5:00 p.m. CST, Monday through Friday. You can also get support by filling out the Web form located at http://247.prenhall.com/mediaform.